CHARLES LATHRAM

Charting the Course

Navigating the Seas of Leadership

First edition

This book was professionally typeset on Reedsy.
Find out more at reedsy.com

Contents

Foreword		v
Preface		xi
Acknowledgement		xvi
1	Navigating the Seas of Leadership	1
2	Commanding the Helm: Autocratic Leadership	25
3	A Crew of Equals: Democratic Leadership	36
4	Charting the Course: Visionary Leadership	44
5	Rising with the Tide: Transformative Leadership	56
6	Putting the Crew First: Servant Leadership	69
7	Charting our Purpose: Why-Based Leadership	82
8	Uniting the Crew: Combined Integrated Leadership Theory	92
9	Walking the Plank of Authenticity: Leading by Example	106
10	Building a Solid Vessel: Creating a Culture of Trust	112
11	Weathering the Storms: Resilience in Leadership	116
12	Charting a Clear Course: Communicating the Vision	119
13	All Hands-on Deck: Empowering Teams	123
14	Junior Officers: Developing Future Captains and Nurturing...	128
15	Steering Through Rough Waters: ...	140

16 Recognizing the Achievements: Cele-
    brating Success   147
17 Sailing into the Sunset: The Legacy of
    the Leader   153
18 Afterword   159

Foreword

As the sun rises over the horizon, the SS Leadership, a ship unlike any other, sets sail on a historic journey. We are not sailing across the oceans of this world but rather the limitless seas of knowledge and leadership; this ship and this journey are unlike any other. As the intrepid explorer, you will embark on a captivating voyage through several leadership philosophies in pursuit of the fundamental principles of effective leadership. Gain a deeper understanding of the fundamental questions that should unify all leadership techniques and the underlying universal currents that govern them all: "Why?" and finally, we will reach our goal: a fresh perspective on leadership—a fresh perspective that goes beyond the constraints of existing theories and introduces a leadership style that is both effective and revolutionary—a style that gives people agency, encourages teamwork, and propels positive change for the benefit of everyone. Our path leads us to this guiding light of inspiration, Combined Integrated Leadership theory, which is genuine, authentic, and motivating. This theory aims to provide a thorough framework for effective leadership in various circumstances by integrating different leadership styles and techniques. However, good leaders understand that there is no such thing as a final destination; instead, they are on a never-ending quest to learn, adapt, and evolve to fulfill the expectations of their organizations, their roles, the environment, and, above all else, the needs of the people they lead.

Welcome, dear voyager, to a narrative unlike any other, a transformative journey that melds the power of experiential learning with the compelling rhythm of a seafaring odyssey. This book, the SS Leadership's log, guides you through intense storms of ideology, calm seas of contemplation, and ports of practice rich with diversity and lessons learned through the ages. As you delve into the pages of this log, you will embark on a voyage that transcends time and space, exploring the depths of leadership philosophy and the intricacies of what motivates human behavior—the essence of leadership. Navigating the treacherous seas of leadership theories and unearthing the hidden knowledge of great leaders from the past can be daunting, but this log will serve as your guide and map the way. As you delve into each page, you'll appreciate the significance of leadership's purpose and meaning in molding the fate of individuals and organizations. To discover the keys to successful leadership, get your sails spread and your thoughts prepared because SS Leadership is about to embark on a life-altering journey.

This ship's decks each highlight distinct approaches and facets of leadership. The inventive mechanisms of the modern world carry us to new heights, while the traditional ways are like sturdy anchors that keep the ship stable amid choppy waters. From the ship's crow's nest, visionary leaders keep an eye out for both possibilities and threats. In the meantime, transactional leaders maintain discipline, efficiency, and order in the engine room, where the ship's wheels and gears enable our voyage. These diverse leadership styles create a stunning symphony of authentic leadership that guides people through the choppy waves of uncertainty. The transformative leaders inspire and encourage the crew as the ship sails through the waves. They advise them to embrace change and contribute to developing an innovative and growing culture. People feel like they own their work and are proud of it when given the resources they need to realize their full potential. This journey of discovery into the qualities of a successful leader demonstrates the potency of several leadership styles working in tandem to steer the ship toward prosperity and success.

With its distinct landscape, echo, and aura, each chapter of this book offers a fresh port of call. Along these picturesque shores, you will find stops where we learn about the lives and legacies of influential people who have left their mark on history. The leadership ideas stored beneath our ship's hull are brought to life in these learning bays through a synthesis of theory and experience that may enlighten even the most seasoned leaders.

Get ready to face calm and turbulent waters head-on as you study transformational leadership's unwavering concentration and servant leadership's balancing currents. Try embracing the long-term thinking of pioneers or investigating the power of balancing cultural, ethical, and team leadership. On your voyage onboard the SS Leadership, you will encounter these and other waterways prepared to lead, test, motivate, and assist you in developing your personal, distinctive concept of leadership. You will navigate the ever-changing tides of leadership, learning to adapt and grow in the face of challenges. As you explore transformational leadership, you will understand the importance of inspiring and motivating your team to achieve greatness. Simultaneously, servant leadership will teach you the value of selflessness and empathy, creating a harmonious and supportive work environment. Embracing long-term thinking will allow you to plan strategically and make informed decisions for the future, while balancing cultural, ethical, and team leadership will help you create a diverse and inclusive organization. Throughout this journey, the SS Leadership will guide you towards becoming a leader who can navigate any waters and inspire others to follow.

Amid a sea of unknowns, this manual will illuminate the way forward. Because a ship without a mission is aimless and meaningless, it gives the crew members something to work toward. A leader's responsibility is to kindle the fire within themselves and their followers, ensuring each individual knows the importance of their voyage. The fundamental principles of leadership are the bedrock upon which all outward manifestations of leadership rest. Examining "why"-based leadership sheds insight on ethical decision-making and personal integrity, as inspiration, motivation, and intention propel leaders to greatness.

However, no leader can successfully traverse the leadership seas on their own. Leadership, like a ship's crew, depends on open lines of communication, cooperation, and confidence. The individual expertise of each member enriches the crew's collective wisdom. Working together, we can face the unknown with poise and strength, for it is through collaboration that we find our way. Every person's opinion matters and is considered in this cooperative setting. Leaders are responsible for encouraging their teams to work harmoniously by creating a climate of trust and open dialogue. With a common goal and an inclusive environment, the crew is strong and ready to weather any storm.

As with any journey, setting sail is not without its risks. Storm clouds may gather on the horizon, threatening to capsize even the sturdiest vessels. Just as a captain faces self-doubt and uncertainty, a leader must weather the storms with resilience and determination. During these tempestuous times, true leadership emerges as they steady the ship and guide their crew safely through the turmoil. A leader must be adaptable and flexible, prepared to change course when necessary. The sea is ever-changing, and challenges arise unexpectedly. A leader must be able to read the winds and currents, adjust their sails, and make timely decisions to ensure the safety and success of the journey. In the depths of the sea, we will find challenges and remarkable treasures waiting to be discovered. A leader must encourage curiosity and innovation within their crew, for it is through exploration and boldness that new ideas and solutions emerge. By fostering a culture of creativity and empowering their team to think outside the box, a leader unlocks the full potential of the collective.

As we embark on this grand adventure, let us also embrace the power of self-reflection. Leaders must continually learn and grow, evaluating their successes and failures to refine their leadership style. As writers revise and edit their work to create a masterpiece, leaders must be open to self-improvement, constantly seeking feedback and development opportunities. Leadership is precious and potent; its essence remains at the core of every journey to success—in business, politics, sports, nonprofits, or education settings—yet let's not mistake leadership for management. While management deals with structure, leadership is about providing direction.

So, my fellow adventurers, let us cast off the lines that tether us to the safety of the harbor. It is time to open our sails, embrace the winds of change, and set sail upon the vast sea of leadership. With courage, dedication, and a bit of saltwater in our veins, we shall embark on a remarkable journey together, facing the unknown with resilience and wisdom. So batten down the hatches and hoist the main sail—the SS Leadership sets off with a promising wind on its ambitious voyage. Prepare to chart your path, to unearth the leader within you, and most importantly, let the titanic seas of leadership knowledge shape your voyage and beyond.

Welcome aboard, voyager! May your journey on the SS Leadership be as enlightening as it is exhilarating. The course for our thrilling expedition into the vast expanse of leadership is set. Anchors aweigh, and away we go!

Preface

Setting Sail

Devotion, Empathy, Integrity, Motivation, and Selflessness are the cardinal points in the compass of our leadership journey. As we embark upon the vast ocean of leadership, this book represents our shared map, where ours is a quest not merely to discover new lands but to explore the depths of leadership styles and distill their essence—an essence that embodies the best traits of all styles folded into one comprehensive amalgamation.

Like seasoned navigators, we will chart our course across vast expanses of the leadership seas, from the autocratic cliffs of firm decision-making through the democratic currents of inclusive team participation to the tranquil depths of purposeful and why-based leadership. Each leadership style represents its unique island in the diverse ocean of guiding principles. Our voyage will take us to the isles of transformative and servant-based leadership, exploring how to shape and serve those we are entrusted to guide, granting them the tools, the engagement, and the belief in a shared vision.

Our ultimate destination lies beyond conventional paradigms. For it is not a singular island or a particular current that we seek but a unified leadership style that integrates the capabilities and attributes of all. We introduce the Combined Integrated Leadership theory, an assemblage of the best traits from all leadership styles—compassionate yet firm, inclusive yet decisive, inspirational yet grounded.

The authentic leader that emerges from this comprehensive theory stands not higher but amongst their team, who listens more than they speak and cultivates not their success, but rather, the success of those they lead. Their primary motivation remains the prosperity and growth of their team because the leader's success is unerringly tied to their team's. In essence, a great leader always puts the needs of others first. In every room they walk into, they're the least important person, and they always eat last at the table of achievements.

This is our journey on the ocean of leadership. Join us as we navigate these waters, casting aside our preconceived notions, uncovering the purist depths of leadership, and steering towards a new era—a new paradigm—of Combined Integrated Leadership. Every captain needs a compass, and this book—this theory—may just be yours. During this voyage, we'll embark on an exciting journey together as we explore the world of leadership. Like setting sail on a vast ocean, leadership can be thrilling and uncertain. But fear not, for I will be your guide, helping you navigate the waves and storms and ultimately steer your ship toward success.

Imagine yourself standing at the helm, feeling the rush of anticipation as the wind catches the sails and propels your vessel forward. As a leader, this moment represents the culmination of countless hours of preparation, planning, and self-reflection. It's a pivotal moment filled with hope and possibility, where the path you choose will shape the course of your journey.

As with any voyage, preparation is key. Before setting sail, you must understand your destination and chart your course. What is the purpose of your leadership journey? Are you aiming to inspire a team to achieve a common goal, positively impact your community, or bring about change on a larger scale? Clarifying your goals and vision will give you direction and help you rally your crew.

Leadership is not a solo effort. Just as a ship cannot sail without a crew, a leader cannot achieve greatness without the support and dedication of their team. A successful leader knows that assembling the right crew, consisting of individuals who possess the necessary skills and share your passion, values, and drive, is essential. Look for diversity within your crew, as this will bring about a wealth of perspectives and ideas, enriching your journey and opening doors to innovative solutions.

Now, as you prepare for this monumental voyage, communication becomes paramount. A leader must be a skilled communicator, capable of articulating their vision and expectations in a way that resonates with their crew. Paint a vivid picture of what lies ahead, inspiring them to join you in this adventure. By fostering a sense of unity and camaraderie and instilling trust and belief in one another, you create an environment that encourages collaboration and fosters a collective commitment to the journey.

However, authentic leadership is more than just issuing orders and expecting others to follow blindly. It is about empowerment. A skilled leader understands the importance of building a culture that allows every crew member to grow and develop their capabilities. Delegate responsibilities, provide the necessary resources and support, and encourage your crew to take ownership of their tasks. This cultivation of individual talents will strengthen your team and cultivate a sense of pride and purpose among its members.

As you set sail into uncharted waters, expect challenges to appear on the horizon. Storms may arise, threatening to disrupt your journey and undermine your progress. But fear not; a skilled leader knows how to weather the storms. Adaptability and resilience become critical traits in these moments. Remain calm, assess the situation, and make informed decisions. Your crew will look to you for guidance and reassurance, and in these testing times, your true leadership capabilities will shine.

Through the pages of this book, we will delve into various leadership styles and strategies, equipping you with the tools needed to navigate the vast ocean of leadership. Each chapter will explore different aspects, from the art of delegation to practical problem-solving, from the importance of empathy to the strength of decisiveness. Through reading and self-reflection, you will gain valuable insights and practical advice, enabling you to steer your ship toward success.

So, my fellow captain, are you ready to set sail on this great leadership adventure? Embrace the unknown, embrace the challenges, and embrace the possibilities that lie ahead. With your passion, dedication, and the knowledge gained from this voyage, there is no limit to what you can achieve as a leader.

Hoist the sails, my friend, and let us embark on this incredible journey together! May fair winds and following seas guide us as we uncover the true essence of leadership and navigate toward a future of growth, excellence, and profound impact.

Acknowledgement

To my wife Jennifer, who has always been my compass, my anchor, and my best friend.

1

Navigating the Seas of Leadership

The immense azure of the water seemed to blend with the deep indigo arc of the horizon as a peaceful evening sank. The coastline was receding further into the distance, becoming a little dot in the vast panorama of the sky and ocean. As the majestic ship sailed into this boundless horizon, our hero, the unstoppable Captain Elara, stood on deck. Amid the crashing waves and terrifying ocean depths, she exuded a calm resolve that echoed with the wind.

With the dreams and ambitions of her crew members on board, Elara gallantly guided a ship over unexplored seas. Elara was not your average leader; on the contrary, she exemplified a distinctive synthesis of leadership philosophies across the whole spectrum: autocratic, democratic, purposeful, why-based, visionary, transformative, and serving. Rather than just traversing an expanse, Elara's voyage across the ocean was a leadership development opportunity. As she navigated treacherous waters, Captain Elara honed her leadership skills and nurtured her crew members' potential. She believed a true leader inspires and empowers others to reach their full potential. Elara saw her voyage as a chance to mold her crew into future leaders, instilling in them the values of courage, resilience, and determination. Each challenge they faced became a valuable lesson in leadership, fostering growth and personal development for all on board.

We all go on a voyage in the sphere of leadership, and it wouldn't be too far-fetched to compare it to crossing a vast ocean. Leadership, after all, is a journey—a difficult walk into uncharted territory through rumbling storms and marveling at perfect dawns. Join us on this exciting journey as we delve into the dynamic realm of leadership. Our fearless captain, Elara, exemplifies the strength, knowledge, and bravery that any great leader should have. We are metaphorically aboard a ship, with our captain, Elara, manning the rudder, preparing to sail into the unknown leadership waters. With her at the helm, we can be sure that a steady hand and a clear vision will steer our journey in the field of leadership. Her strength will keep us resilient in the face of adversity, her knowledge will illuminate the path ahead, and her bravery will inspire us to push beyond our limits. As we set sail into uncharted waters, we can't help but feel a sense of excitement and anticipation for the transformative journey that lies before us. Together, with Elara's leadership, we are ready to navigate the unpredictable storms and celebrate the glorious victories that await us on this exhilarating adventure.

Like our journey to become wise, effective, and prosperous leaders, hers is full of ups and downs. Elara's life experiences provide valuable comparisons. She exemplifies resiliency by facing the violent fury of the waves. She highlights the need for a leader's commitment to lifelong learning and strategic planning during starry evenings spent contemplating and plotting. Her journey is a testament to the power of perseverance and determination, as she has encountered numerous obstacles and challenges. Elara's ability to adapt and learn from these experiences has shaped her into the exceptional leader she is today. As we embark on this transformative journey, we will draw inspiration from her wisdom and guidance, knowing that with her at the helm, we are equipped to weather any storm and reach new heights of success and growth. The starry evenings spent contemplating and plotting symbolize her dedication to continuous improvement and strategic thinking, reminding us of the importance of always striving for excellence in our leadership journeys.

Remember that Elara is a guide, not a guarantee, during the maze-like voyage, even though she embodies leadership. You may have had a subtle, one-of-a-kind journey filled with personal triumphs and tribulations. Unexpected turbulence or stunning views might be on the horizon. But the lessons learned from Elara's journey—the perseverance through chaos, the serenity in stillness, and the planning for the unknown—can help you find your way. No two leadership journeys are the same, and Elara's story reminds us that we must navigate our maze-like voyages with determination and adaptability. While Elara embodies leadership qualities, she also teaches us that there are no guarantees in this journey, and we must be prepared for unexpected challenges and opportunities. By embracing the lessons from Elara's journey, such as perseverance, serenity, and strategic planning, we can better equip ourselves to find our path to excellence and success.

We warmly welcome you to join us, esteemed reader and fellow voyager. Get ready to set sail on your adventure, ride the refreshing sea wind, and navigate the hypnotic landscape of leadership as we explore its intriguing intersection, one wave at a time. We trust our skipper to lead the way as we set sail.

At the head of her ship, Elara looks out over the vast horizon, her imagination filling in the blanks with visions of uncharted territories and limitless potential. She rallied her crew behind a common aim by bringing forth their shared desire. To hone her visionary abilities even further, Elara studied the stars and stories of long-gone explorers; she eventually became adept at conveying her fascinating vision to her crew passionately and clearly. Elara's passion and clarity inspired her crew, who eagerly absorbed her lessons and showed loyalty to their captain. The crew became more cohesive as time passed because they all believed in the potential of exploration and the endless possibilities that lay ahead. As they embarked on their journey, Elara's ability to articulate her vision became the guiding force that propelled the ship forward, navigating through uncharted waters with unwavering determination. Together, they embarked on a voyage of discovery, ready to uncover the world's mysteries and embrace the boundless potential that awaited them.

As a servant leader, Captain Elara encouraged her team to work together. Working as a team had made her hands calloused, but she was well-versed in every square inch of the ship, including the deck, sails, and knots. She compassionately attended to her crew members' needs and exhibited servant leadership by empathizing with their stories of joy and sorrow. To develop these qualities, she was humble enough to put others' needs before hers. Captain Elara believed that authentic leadership meant putting the needs of her crew before her own. She understood that by being humble and selfless, she could create a supportive and cohesive team. She knew that her role as a servant leader was not just about giving orders but about genuinely caring for and understanding her crew members. By doing so, Captain Elara fostered a sense of trust and loyalty among her team, ensuring they were not just colleagues but a family united in their pursuit of discovery and potential.

Through thick and thin, calm and storm, our captain is a change agent who teaches and encourages her crew to do the same. Elara pushed her colleagues to think outside the box and create an atmosphere where change was the only constant, accentuating her transformational qualities. Elara's leadership was firmly centered on the 'why.' This style of leadership guided her to make decisions and take action. To hone this quality even more, Elara reflected on herself and thought of others to ensure their courses stayed on track with their overall goal. She constantly reminded herself and her crew of the bigger picture, reminding them of the purpose and vision behind their work. Elara believed understanding the 'why' was crucial in inspiring and motivating her team to push boundaries and achieve greatness. By constantly reaffirming their purpose, Elara ensured everyone remained focused and driven despite challenges and setbacks. Her dedication to staying on course with their overall goal created a sense of unity and determination among her crew, ultimately leading to their success in pursuing discovery and potential.

The compass that Elara followed was purposeful leadership. There was complete mission alignment in every action, command, and rudder adjustment. Elara cultivated this characteristic by making deliberate decisions that influenced her trip, considering immediate and longer-term consequences. She understood that purposeful leadership required short-term success and long-term sustainability. Elara encouraged open communication and collaboration, ensuring every crew member felt heard and valued. She recognized the importance of empowering her team, allowing them to take ownership of their roles and contribute their unique skills and perspectives. By fostering a culture of trust and respect, Elara created an environment where everyone felt motivated to give their best, even when faced with adversity. Her purposeful leadership guided them through the challenges of their journey and inspired each individual to grow and develop personally and professionally.

Under Elara's guidance, the crew members became more confident in their abilities and began to unlock their full potential. She provided opportunities for professional development and encouraged them to pursue their passions and interests. This resulted in a team that was not only highly skilled and efficient but also passionate and engaged. Elara's impactful leadership style left a lasting impression on each crew member, instilling a sense of pride and accomplishment for contributing to the mission's success.

Her blended leadership style was simultaneously advantageous and challenging. Because of her inclusive and collaborative personality, Elara may take her time to respond decisively when the situation calls for it, which might be problematic when confronted with dangerous situations requiring rapid responses, such as pirate raids or dangerous waters. One of the keys to effective leadership, which she recognized, is the capacity to pivot quickly and easily. She showed remarkable agility in responding to changing circumstances by fluidly switching between leadership styles: servant when her team needed assistance, visionary when their purpose faded, transformer when traditional approaches failed, and purposeful leader when the road ahead got murky. Her ability to adapt her leadership style to the needs of her team was awe-inspiring. She knew how to lead by providing guidance and support during challenging times or inspiring her team with a clear vision and direction. This versatility allowed her to navigate the murky waters of uncertainty and make decisive decisions when necessary. Her agility in switching between leadership styles proved invaluable, especially when confronted with dangerous situations like pirate raids. Ultimately, her capacity to pivot quickly and easily made her an exceptional leader that her team could always rely on. For example, during a pirate raid on their cargo ship, she immediately switched to an authoritative leadership style, coordinating the evacuation and defensive actions precisely. Simultaneously, she remained calm and composed, encouraging and reassuring her team in the face of danger. Her ability to adapt her leadership style in such a high-stakes situation protected her crew and showcased her exceptional leadership skills under extreme pressure.

Elara, our skipper, set sail on an everlasting leadership development journey. She led her crew across a vast and treacherous ocean using a variety of leadership approaches, creating a legacy of togetherness, purpose, and change that would last for years to come. One of Elara's most formative experiences at sea was the epiphany that great leaders don't hail from the quarterdeck but rather guide their crews' emotions toward an exhilarating future with unwavering resolve. She understood that leadership was not just about giving orders and making decisions but about inspiring and empowering her crew. She realized that by fostering a sense of togetherness and purpose, she could create a motivated and united team to overcome any obstacle. Through her unwavering resolve, Elara guided her crew's emotions and instilled in them a shared vision of an exhilarating future where they could conquer the challenges of the ocean and achieve greatness together. This realization marked a turning point in Elara's leadership journey, propelling her to become an exceptional and influential leader.

Despite the ups and downs of her voyage, Captain Elara's leadership was as extensive and profound as the sea. Her adaptability helped her lead the ship and crew through challenging times when integrated leadership methods failed. This demonstrated the breadth and depth of her leadership. Elara reverted to her collaborative methods, listening for crew voices when calm waters and good breezes returned; when rapid action was necessary, she employed decisive command with clear commands. Elara emphasized the need for her and her crew to develop physical and mental courage. In the face of uncertainty, Elara and her team faced their mistakes, questioned long-held assumptions, and persevered through tough times because of their bravery. Elara exemplified leadership through servant-hardheartedness, visionary foresight, transformational resilience, conviction founded on why, and purposeful navigation. Elara's servant-hardheartedness was evident in her dedication to the well-being and growth of her crew. She always put their needs before hers, ensuring they were well cared for and supported in their personal and professional development.

Additionally, her visionary foresight allowed her to anticipate challenges and opportunities, enabling her to make informed decisions that would benefit the entire team. Elara's transformational resilience was a testament to her ability to adapt and bounce back from setbacks, inspiring her crew to do the same. Her conviction, founded on a deep understanding of why they were on this mission, gave her the strength to lead with unwavering determination and inspire her crew to stay focused and motivated.

Finally, Elara's purposeful navigation ensured that every crew member went above and beyond as sailors; they exemplified the leadership that can unite a group against a common enemy. They learned that leadership is not something to be hoarded but relatively freely given; leadership is rich in the small things: acts of kindness, shared dreams, accepted changes, and necessary steps toward their objective. They quickly learned that the trip itself—growing as individuals, facing obstacles directly, and developing into leaders under Elara's guidance—was more important than any specific physical objective they may have had. Her direction highlighted the difficulties they encountered and the opportunities each person had.

"Charting the Course" does not provide a how-to guide for perfect leadership. Instead, it uncovers the core of leadership via personal stories, reflections, and anecdotes. Leadership is like navigating the blue, unpredictable waters; you must recognize your talents and limitations and find your way. Elara's guidance in "Charting the Course" emphasizes the importance of self-awareness and self-reflection in leadership. The book encourages readers to understand their strengths and weaknesses and embrace the unpredictability and challenges of being a leader. By sharing personal stories and anecdotes, Elara helps readers realize that leadership is not about following a set formula but finding their unique path and making the most of their abilities. Ultimately, "Charting the Course" teaches that authentic leadership comes from within and that individuals can navigate the turbulent waters of leadership with confidence and success by understanding themselves.

Every adventure begins with a single stride, or in this instance, a courageous push against the powerful waves, so keep that in mind as we set sail. Elara's path was endless and expansive, like the ocean itself: with every wave came a new lesson, with every star a symbol, and with every day came a new opportunity for her to grow as a leader. Even though her trip was unique, those who participated will never forget it. It serves as a reminder that true leaders are responsible for more than just the physical well-being of their followers; they must also handle their followers' spirits with wisdom and compassion, all in the name of steadfast dedication to the journey as a whole.

Sailing over the enormous leadership seas, we must constantly adjust to the shifting tides of possibilities and threats. We are responsible for leading our team and company to victory, much like a ship's captain.

Leadership is an art form that requires skill in navigating by plotting a path and knowing the waters we'll be sailing through. With this knowledge, we may react wisely to the ever-changing factors influencing our path. Market developments, technical breakthroughs, socio-political dynamics, and other external influences shape the complex and ever-changing leadership landscape. Culture, values, and the collective psyche of our team members are internal currents within our companies that also significantly impact our journey.

Keeping yourself informed and adaptable is critical for navigating these currents. Much like a captain, a leader's job is to keep a weather eye on the world around them, looking for danger or opportunity. To achieve this goal, it is necessary to cultivate an environment where employees are curious about new things and willing to adapt and keep up with trends in the sector. A growth mentality equips leaders to weather leadership storms with grace and agility, resolving issues as they arise.

As leaders, we often encounter a wide variety of complicated external currents. Interest rates, inflation, and currency exchange rates are just a few examples of the factors that could affect the economic ebb and flow our organizations are susceptible to. Other unanticipated obstacles that could shift the trajectory of company operations include changes in regulations and geopolitical concerns. Digital transformation

11

and innovation are also necessary for leaders to remain ahead of technological upheavals, which may create seismic shifts in sectors. To navigate these external currents and ensure the success of our companies, leaders must possess agility and adaptability. This means quickly responding to changes in interest rates, inflation, currency exchange rates, regulations, and geopolitical concerns. Additionally, embracing digital transformation and fostering a culture of innovation can help leaders stay ahead of disruptions and proactively identify growth opportunities.

Still, we can't afford to ignore anything that isn't an external current. Equally potent can be the internal dynamics of our enterprises. The culture we foster shapes each team member's path. A culture that encourages open dialogue, teamwork, and adaptability is something that leaders should work to create and nurture. Leaders can build a strong and inspired team by fostering an atmosphere that welcomes different perspectives and values various opinions. By embracing diversity and encouraging collaboration, leaders can tap into their team's collective intelligence, leading to more innovative solutions and a better understanding of market trends. Furthermore, fostering adaptability within the organization allows for quick adjustments to changing circumstances and ensures that the company can respond effectively to technological disruptions. Ultimately, a strong and inspired team empowered to challenge the status quo will be better equipped to navigate the ever-evolving business landscape and seize new growth opportunities.

Another thing that effective leaders know is that there's more to the sea than just the currents. We confront complicated and intricate problems, and the depth of the water reflects that. It takes cautious navigation to avoid hazards and impediments when encountering shallow seas. Situations require rigorous analysis as we strive for a detailed comprehension of the intricacies. This requires attentive listening to those with a stake in the outcome, careful analysis, and including multiple viewpoints in the decision-making process. To make educated decisions and prevent catastrophic outcomes, leaders must delve deeply.

Difficulties are an inherent aspect of navigating the leadership seas. Similar to how a captain needs to be ready for stormy weather, leaders need to be able to handle difficult situations. Crisis management, making difficult decisions under pressure, and being calm in the face of hardship are all part of this. When leaders are genuine and open with their team, they build trust and confidence, which helps them weather the storms together. When leaders embrace multiple viewpoints in decision-making, they create an environment that fosters innovation and creativity. By considering diverse perspectives, leaders can identify blind spots and potential pitfalls, leading to more well-rounded and informed decisions. Additionally, involving team members in the decision-making process enhances their sense of ownership and commitment and allows for a broader range of expertise to be utilized. Ultimately, by encouraging open dialogue and valuing different opinions, leaders can cultivate a resilient and adaptable team that can navigate any challenges that come their way.

On the other hand, chances for transformation might emerge

during storms. A crisis is an opportunity for leaders to learn and innovate; therefore, they must embrace it and maximize the situation. Unexpected opportunities and latent potential are frequently exposed during times of turmoil. Leaders may motivate their teams to accept change and adapt when faced with challenges by creating an atmosphere encouraging experimentation and learning. The company can reach heights it never thought possible with this kind of nimbleness and readiness to take measured risks. By fostering a culture of resilience and embracing change, leaders can inspire their teams to view obstacles as stepping stones toward growth and success. Encouraging an open mindset and emphasizing the importance of continuous learning enables individuals to unleash their hidden talents and capabilities. Through calculated risks and a willingness to explore new avenues, organizations can seize unforeseen opportunities and propel themselves toward unprecedented achievements. Ultimately, a team that is adaptable and fearless in the face of challenges will survive and thrive in the ever-evolving business landscape.

It is easy to become bogged down by the difficulties of leading at sea and forget why we are here. We must establish a distinct goal for our business so that we can all work together towards it. A compelling vision unites the group's efforts and motivates them to achieve a common goal. But vision without purpose, without knowing why we do what we do, is insufficient. Passion, self-determination, and the ability to overcome challenges are all enhanced when the crew has a clear sense of purpose. The leader is responsible for conveying and emphasizing this goal to the team so that everyone believes in it and is motivated to give their all no matter what comes their way.

The leadership seas are stormy; no captain can weather them alone. Leadership that succeeds requires collaboration and teamwork. Leaders should create a setting where different viewpoints are valued, and ideas are shared openly. Leaders may harness their crew's collective intelligence by establishing an environment of psychological safety where everyone feels comfortable speaking up and sharing what they know. As a consequence of working together, team members feel more invested in the organization's goals and can better contribute to decision-making. This collaborative approach to leadership fosters a sense of ownership and empowerment among team members, as they feel valued and respected for their contributions. By embracing diverse perspectives and encouraging open communication, leaders can tap into their team's wealth of knowledge and expertise, leading to more informed and effective decision-making. Ultimately, this collaborative leadership style strengthens the team and enables the organization to navigate the storms of the leadership seas with greater agility and resilience.

Our duty as leaders is to bravely and expertly traverse the leadership waters. We may navigate towards triumph by being aware of and adaptable to the winds and currents, gracefully enduring storms, seizing chances for development and innovation, establishing a distinct goal and purpose, and encouraging teamwork among our members. If we can conquer the navigational challenges of leadership, a better future for our organizations and the people we lead may be shaped.

Leadership styles such as autocracy, democracy, visionary leadership, and servant leadership will be examined in this story, focusing on their core characteristics and complexities. Consider several purpose-driven leadership styles, such as transformational, values-led, and "why-based" approaches. Each leadership style has its advantages, and followers should be able to identify them. By understanding the core characteristics and complexities of different leadership styles, we can foster a culture of open-mindedness and collaboration within our organizations. Transformational leadership, for example, inspires and motivates employees to go beyond their self-interests and work towards a common goal. Values-led leadership ensures that ethical principles guide decision-making processes, fostering trust and integrity among team members. Lastly, a "why-based" approach focuses on articulating the purpose and mission of the organization, creating a sense of meaning and direction for all involved. By embracing these purpose-driven leadership styles, we can empower our followers to identify and appreciate each style's unique advantages, leading to a stronger and more prosperous future for our companies and those we lead.

We may combine the contrasting theoretical frameworks for understanding leadership with these intriguing branches of leadership studies. If that's the case, we could finally have a game-changing hypothesis. When these crucial elements come together, the result is an experience that motivates revolutionary change rather than merely inducing it. Leadership styles such as visionary, servant, transformational, purpose-led, values-led, and "why-based" can be combined to build an all-encompassing strategy that motivates revolutionary change. This all-encompassing strategy will bring about transformation, offer our team tangible advantages, and give them direction. With this idea in hand, we can completely alter the course of events and design a transformative leadership program.

A leader's role is similar to that of a symphony conductor in that they have an impact on others around them. They need to have goals and ideals that underpin their oracular vision, and most importantly, they need to have the guts to ask and answer the "why" behind every "what." A tyrant with the compassion of a servant and the poise of a symphony in charge. It should motivate, inspire, and unite everyone with whom it interacts.

This book aims to distinguish between "management" and "leadership" and shed light on the common confusion between the two. In contrast to management's emphasis on distributing and supervising resources to achieve specific objectives, leadership is concerned with inspiring and persuading followers to follow a vision willingly. Although they call for distinct skills and approaches, management and leadership are equally critical to an organization's success. In addition to providing guidance and direction, trustworthy leaders inspire teamwork, delegate responsibility, and earn subordinates' confidence. Conversely, good managers are masters at arranging, planning, and solving difficulties to get things done quickly. However, all groups and organizations that achieve lasting success share one thing in common: they are led with a strong sense of purpose, rooted in values, and the "why" behind their work is evident in every aspect of the company. Inspiring, shaping, and sharing this audacious vision requires our combined efforts.

17

Unlike any other voyage, it will provide you with information, insights, and experiences you will never regret. This audacious vision will push you to explore new ideas, take calculated risks, and challenge the status quo. It will empower you to make a difference and leave a lasting impact on the world. As we embark on this journey together, we will face obstacles and setbacks, but our shared sense of purpose will keep us resilient and determined. So, let us unite, bring our strengths and talents to the table, and create a future we can all be proud of.

Rising with the sun is a long, lean figure on the horizon, about to go on a grand voyage. The foundation of this incredible ship is a set of four principles as vast as the ocean: trust, openness, communication, and vision. Come along with us as we face challenges head-on and embrace opportunities as we embark on a thrilling journey to become seasoned leaders.

A skipper maintains her equilibrium while staring out to sea while standing at the ship's bow. This character shows the importance of exploring all available paths rather than being satisfied with only reaching their destination. Being a leader is more than just filling a function; it should be about building a life around what you can do better.

Like water, which is subject to multiple currents that alter its trajectory over time, leadership is fundamentally complex and ever-changing. This trip will explore authoritarian, democratic, visionary, transformational (from servant to servant leadership), purposeful, and why-based approaches to leadership. Mastering the art of elegantly riding each wave is crucial for cultivating a leadership practice that takes full advantage of the ebb and flow.

A strong wind is propelling the ship of an autocratic leader relentlessly. Furthermore, democratic leadership mimics the natural process of variety and unity by soliciting feedback from successive waves. Like north stars, leaders with vision point the way and aren't afraid to reveal their emotions. Humility and service are a servant leader's lifeblood, like the ship's hull that keeps those aboard safe. On the other hand, transformational, why-based, or purposeful leaders are always trying new things to grow as people or achieve significant goals.

According to the innovative Combined Integrated Leadership theory, these leadership ideas are not islands unto themselves but rather components of a continuous shoreline lit by a lighthouse. From the inside out, the best leaders may be developed by constructing a philosophy that deftly combines the critical elements of several leadership styles. Like a seasoned helmsman steadily navigating tricky waters, this would require delicate juggling between several genres.

What you will see in the following chapters is just the tip of the iceberg. In the next sections, we will explore each leadership style more deeply, explaining the why and what of each idea. No matter what the future brings, I am ready to soak up all the knowledge I can and savor every minute. Taking charge is like entering a beautiful, intricate, and expansive new universe.

Leadership, however, must be defined. Is it small enough to fit inside a clearly defined box? Most likely not, although there are commonalities and a core concept acts as motivation, inspiration, or the "why." Leadership is a complex and multi-faceted concept that cannot be confined to a narrow definition or specific characteristics. It is a dynamic and ever-evolving phenomenon encompassing various styles, approaches, and ideologies. While there may be commonalities and a central underlying principle that drives leadership, it is essential to recognize that it can manifest in diverse ways depending on the context and individual preferences. Therefore, embracing the expansiveness of leadership allows us to explore its intricacies and tap into its vast potential for personal and organizational growth.

A leader's impact is like the ripples in an ocean; they may be felt everywhere and at any moment. The excitement and satisfaction of unraveling its secrets stem from the fresh understanding it offers of this worldwide occurrence. Before moving forward, we must clarify what leadership is not. An outstanding leader can inspire followers to reach their full potential while guiding them towards a common goal. Having official authority over team members is less important than fostering trust, cooperation, and mutual respect. Once we've gotten the hang of these basics, we can explore several leadership styles to find the one that suits us or our company the best.

The ability to guide others toward a goal, alter their perspective, and motivate them to take action is known as influence, and it is the bedrock of leadership. Imagine a leader who wants to achieve collective goals without using control, manipulation, or force. If that's the case, they need to figure out how to inspire their followers to tackle those goals with all their might and determination.

Assessing and prioritizing one's strengths and weaknesses is the initial stage in honing one's leadership abilities. This encompasses traits such as being forthright, empathetic, and persistent. Would you rather have a more autocratic leader, like a ship's captain, who uses force to keep things running smoothly, or someone who is more democratic, like an orchestra director, who encourages collaboration and consensus-building when making decisions?

Striding fearlessly into unknown realms, like legendary explorers, are we visionary leaders with plans for the future? What if, on the other hand, we acted as selfless servant leaders and demonstrated to our followers how to take care of a flower?

Are we better suited to a transformational leadership style, guiding our charges to reach their full potential and create a positive impact, or are we more of an inspiring coaching approach? Is our approach more in line with "why?"-based leadership, in which a leader periodically asks, "Why?" to direct a group toward an objective?

All of these ways enhance the leadership fabric. On the other hand, a fascinating new notion is buried deep inside it. Coming together like a lighthouse, the Combined Integrated Leadership theory aspires to harmonize these leadership tenets, explaining the reasoning behind our day-to-day decisions.

This narrative journey aims to help us adapt to different surroundings, situations, and the people we lead by exploring and evaluating our inherent leadership style. Subsequent chapters shift from focusing on leadership to examining our identities.

We invite you to join us to explore these intriguing leadership philosophies, which will conclude with an introduction to the Combined Integrated Leadership theory. I am thrilled to embark on this thrilling journey of self-exploration and mastering the fundamentals of leadership! On this adventure, though, where precisely ought we to set out? The blueprints for our ship must take precedence.

Step aboard the SS Leadership, our symbol of leadership, and we'll cruise across the vast leadership chasm. A strong vessel is necessary for navigating the treacherous seas of influential people, groups, and communities. From authoritarian to democratic to servant to transformational leadership, it needs preparation, the right resources, and an unmistakable vision. The concept of "why"—the existential force that motivates our thoughts and actions—and purposeful leadership are at the heart of all the accessible resources.

The many sections of our ship stand for various leadership philosophies. Authoritarianism is like a cold steel cutlass: it's all about rapid choices and strong commands. The democratic method promotes free speech and collective decision-making like pliable yet durable rubber. A servant leader is unwavering in their commitment to prioritizing the needs of their team members before their own. Like state-of-the-art navigational tools, transformational leaders skillfully launch and oversee change while inspiring followers with our vision.

The "why" question is integral to our ship's wheel since it may help us determine where our inspiration originates. Our SS Leadership is robust even in the face of challenging times because this "why" unites us in our objectives, gives our activities meaning, and guides us to our final destinations. Choosing the right materials for a ship's various sections is just as crucial as choosing a style that suits one's personality. Leaders who are good at encouraging and guiding reasonable debates may thrive under a more democratic form of leadership, as opposed to leaders who are hasty to form opinions and prefer an authoritarian management style.

Improving one's approach to leadership is an ongoing process. Putting in time to study, practice, reflect, and critique. As a first step, one should be self-aware regarding their leadership style, principles, vision, and "why" (the reason behind their actions). Listening to other people's opinions is a great way to get perspective and find places to improve. Everyone, from bosses to subordinates to peers, is a part of this. You can gain theoretical knowledge and practical skills through mentoring, leadership development programs, and publications. In this comparison, an experienced sailor may be a guide, imparting knowledge gained from a lifetime of exploration through advice, tactics, and techniques.

Leadership qualities such as attentive listening, perseverance, empathy, and decisiveness may be honed with time and effort. Recognizing and controlling one's own emotions, as well as those of other people, is a crucial component of emotional intelligence. Learning to navigate a ship safely is like being an expert wave reader. It requires understanding the patterns and behaviors of waves, anticipating their movements, and making calculated decisions to ensure a smooth and successful journey. Similarly, developing emotional intelligence involves recognizing and interpreting the subtle cues and signals in human interactions, allowing individuals to navigate relationships and situations skillfully and with finesse. Both skills require practice, experience, and a deep understanding of the elements at play.

Remember that leadership growth is like ship maintenance—a continuous process. We may forge on fearlessly toward our objective, even if the waters may be rough. Onboard the formidable SS Leadership, we shall fearlessly cry, "Ahoy, horizon, here we come!"

Now we may begin, respected reader! Leaders encourage us to delve into the unknown by questioning long-held beliefs and practices to build a better future together. It is a pleasure to welcome you here today.

2

Commanding the Helm: Autocratic Leadership

The Journey:

As she readied her ship for the voyage, the navigator faced the chill of an early winter morning. The onlookers watched as the squeaks and cracks in the wood melted away in her skilled hands. Amidst the cool air, crew members who were half-awake after long hours of travel massaged their eyes and exhaled steam.

Her unwavering stare and commanding voice made the navigator stand out as no ordinary captain. Imagine her strong hand firmly grasping the ship's structural helm. At the beginning of their expedition, her vision and command dictated the course of action, and her words resounded through the air, expressing the true essence of authoritarian leadership.

Our Navigator personifies authoritarian leadership as an unwavering lighthouse that beckons and guides. Amid anarchy, it forms a steady, unblinking beam rather than a comical lighthouse that flickers erratically.

As the crewmen obey without inquiry, strong hands steer the ship over heavy seas. In instances where time is of the essence and mistakes might have catastrophic consequences, autocratic leadership can be effective. Quick thinking and decisive action are hallmarks of an autocratic leader who can set their team on the path to success with pinpoint accuracy.

Let us not romanticize the idea; innovation suffers under an authoritarian leader since he or she values compliance more than his or her original thought. It would be reassuring and secure to cruise over unending calm seas, but how can the crew grow without the constant disturbance of waves? To face new challenges, how will the ship change and adapt?

When the going gets tough, an authoritarian leader may rally the troops to overcome obstacles like rough waters or pressing deadlines. However, during relative peace and exploration periods, when fresh avenues for invention present themselves, a dictatorial style of leadership risks immobilizing the ship and its crew while leaving the ocean floor unexplored.

Leadership is not a zero-sum game; its strength is its adaptability. Mastery requires delving into each style as if they were wind currents that may carry us to uncharted territories or shield us from impending doom. Sailing successfully or disastrously depends on knowing when and which winds to use.

Why does authoritarian leadership work the way it does? Let's find out. What causes it to flourish in specific environments while appearing parched in others? Why is it so good at navigating rough seas yet less so when the weather is calm? We need to know "what" autocratic leadership does and "why" it does it if we want to comprehend it fully.

As we go forward, it's wise to be alert like our navigator would be; different leadership styles provide different experiences, lessons, and stories. There are many different kinds of leadership, and autocratic leadership is just one. Let's keep digging into the ocean of leadership and discovering all its secrets.

The "What(s)" of Autocratic Leadership

Leadership sparks the flame of organizational success by fueling innovation, promoting growth, and amplifying employee productivity. Autocratic or authoritarian leadership is characterized by individual control over all decisions with little input from group members. Autocrats tend to make decisions based on their ideas and judgment, not accepting advice from followers. Instead, they micromanage all work processes and techniques, widely regarded as controlling and bossy.

Organizations with a vertical structure prioritizing clear lines of authority, well-defined responsibilities, and close hierarchical cooperation are ideal environments for autocratic leadership styles. A steady hand at the helm is essential for ships fighting rough waters or navigating complicated regulations. Everyone must be on the same page regarding the leader's decisions and how to implement them for alignment to stay. Feedback channels should be in place, so staff input is not entirely ignored, and friction is not exacerbated. It works wonders in establishments like fast food joints, military bases, and factories that rely heavily on routine and structure to ensure maximum productivity. Because the leader is solely responsible for making choices, procedures move more quickly, resulting in fewer delays and speedier actions.

For instance, a real-world application is seen within Apple Inc., particularly under the leadership of the late Steve Jobs. His vision and micromanagement style helped foster innovation and elevate the company to unprecedented heights in the technology sector.

Another stark example is Martha Stewart's enterprise's success. Stewart consistently maintained an autocratic leadership style, allowing her to own and control her brand's aesthetic and ensure that all products stayed true to her desired image and quality.

The benefits of an autocratic leadership style aren't without their downsides. Because employees aren't involved in making decisions, morale takes a nosedive, and a dependent culture develops. Staff members may feel dissatisfied with an autocratic leader's management style and decide to leave the company altogether. The authoritarian management style of Steve Jobs, in contrast to Apple's success, was criticized for fostering an atmosphere of high pressure and low morale among employees. Employees reported low levels of job satisfaction due to frequent feelings of being undervalued and excluded from decision-making.

Although autocratic leadership styles have drawbacks, they also have their uses and circumstances in which they thrive. To hone your autocratic leadership abilities, consider the following:

Keeping the lines of communication open is the first and foremost priority. Autocratic leaders must be direct and to the point when giving commands or setting expectations. To facilitate a smooth workflow, leaders should ensure their communication is straightforward. In a totalitarian setting, trust is paramount. Leaders may boost productivity by building trust with their staff by demonstrating expertise, knowledge, and a desire to improve.

Effective autocratic leaders must balance autocracy with empathy. Balancing a firm grip with empathy can improve work satisfaction, even amidst stringent regulations. A vital aspect is respecting employees and understanding their perspectives, which can reduce employee turnover rates.

Though decision-making lies entirely with the leader, integrating regular feedback sessions and recognizing employee accomplishments can boost morale and encourage a positive work environment. Gaining feedback from peers, superiors, and subordinates can help identify areas for improvement. Regular training and workshops can also aid in developing and reinforcing leadership abilities.

Additionally, leaders should not anchor down to a single leadership style; instead, an adaptable approach is more advantageous. A robust leader navigates different styles like a seasoned captain, maneuvering their ship based on the wind's direction (situational challenges) and destination (organizational goals).

Autocratic leadership stands apart from other forms of leadership when compared to them. A fundamental tenet of theories of leadership known as "why-based" or "purposeful" leadership is the idea that leaders should know and share the organization's fundamental purpose with their teams so that they can rally around it in times of crisis and act swiftly. By stressing this meaningful message, leaders utilizing this style may inspire their teams to make swift decisions and give their work significance and worth. This method of inspiration and buy-in from everyone involved is easy to understand and implement. To motivate and engage followers, leaders who operate on a "why" basis must explain the rationale behind their objectives. Finally, leaders who practice purposeful leadership see themselves as ambassadors for the organization's stated goals and objectives.

Democratic leaders promote a sense of shared accountability by soliciting team opinions before making decisions. Because they are more concerned with serving than leading, servant leaders prioritize their team's development and happiness in an environment of mutual respect and collaboration. However, there are instances where servant leadership may prioritize personal needs ahead of the organization's bigger picture.

The transformative leadership philosophy centers on changing things as they are and building a shared vision for the future. Transformational leaders utilize idealized influence, intellectual stimulation, personal attention, and inspiring motivation to change how people think and act in a company. This approach may bring about profound change, but it demands a lot of work and talent and may meet with opposition.

As we thread these various leadership styles together, the best deciphering becomes crucial for any aspiring leader. It would necessitate a thorough introspection of their personality, values, and strengths while considering the organizational culture, group dynamics, and nature of tasks. To aid with this, we will provide a road map for leadership development throughout our exploration. We will provide practical advice, actionable feedback, and strategic tools designed to make you the most competent leader you can be.

A leader's effectiveness depends on several factors, including organizational culture and needs, the type of work the team performs, the employees' skills, and the leader's style and abilities. No one leadership style is always the best option in every situation. Leaders should assess their convictions, qualities, and scenarios they'll likely encounter. They should also be open to adapting, understanding the utility of other leadership styles, and developing specific traits—authoritative clarity, decision-making skill, or empathy, among others—to enrich their leadership repertoire.

Within the context of a ship, the autocratic leader takes command of the helm, guiding the vessel through the vast and treacherous waters. Like the captain, who makes critical decisions and expects immediate obedience from the crew, the autocratic leader believes that their vision and expertise are paramount and that their decisions should not be questioned.

Strong self-assurance in one's decision-making ability is a hallmark of autocratic leadership. Because of their extensive knowledge and expertise in their field, they can quickly assess complicated circumstances and act decisively. Situations when the leader's knowledge is unmatched or where time for discussion is at a premium lend themselves well to this approach. The authoritarian leader's quick and well-considered actions in such a situation can provide desirable results.

However, autocratic leadership can also have its drawbacks. By relying solely on their own judgment, autocratic leaders may overlook valuable insights and perspectives from their crew members. This approach can stifle creativity and innovation, as individuals may feel discouraged from contributing ideas or raising concerns.

Furthermore, the crew may lose faith in the authoritarian leader due to his or her obsession with power and control. Disempowerment and undervaluation among team members can lead to a decline in motivation and dedication to the objective, impacting the ship's overall performance and morale.

The key to effective autocratic leadership is striking a balance between the leader's authoritative position and the crew's demands. Establishing trust and encouraging open lines of communication is essential to mitigating some of the risks associated with this leadership style. Even an authoritarian leader may make good judgments with the help of their team's knowledge and experience if they ask for and consider their opinions and suggestions often.

Additionally, authoritarian leaders should be aware that there are times when a more collaborative and adaptable approach is needed. Being flexible and prepared to take on responsibility when the time is right may foster an upbeat and productive atmosphere on board.

Combining autocratic and servant leadership styles is one way to overcome autocratic leadership's shortcomings. Empathy, attentive listening, and encouragement of team development and success are hallmarks of servant leadership. A more welcoming and inspiring workplace may be achieved when an authoritarian leader applies servant leadership concepts. An authoritarian leader may build trust and involvement by showing genuine interest in his or her crew's goals and desires, giving everyone a stake in the mission's outcome. This shift in leadership style can create a collaborative and supportive environment where team members feel valued and empowered. An authoritarian leader can foster a sense of belonging and motivate their team to work towards a common goal by incorporating servant leadership principles. Ultimately, this approach can lead to increased productivity, employee satisfaction, and overall success for the organization.

In addition, situational leadership may work for authoritarian leaders as well. Adapting one's leadership style to fit a given circumstance is something that situational leadership acknowledges. Autocratic leaders may adjust to different situations and ensure their success by knowing when to be more autocratic and when to be more democratic or laissez-faire.

When swift action and unambiguous guidance are needed, authoritarian leadership may work wonders in a crisis. By imposing his will on the group, an authoritarian leader can keep everyone on target and prevent them from getting lost in the mayhem. Because of their swift decision-making and forceful personalities, autocratic leaders reassure their crews that someone is in charge and understands what to do.

Even an authoritarian leader should consider becoming more collaborative when dealing with an exceptionally competent team or when confronted with a difficult situation that calls for fresh ideas. By promoting candid discussion, ideation, and participation, the leader may harness the combined wisdom of the crew and bring fresh viewpoints to the table. The crew feels more invested and accountable in the process as a whole, which boosts engagement and productivity.

Groups that must adhere rigidly to rules and regulations, like emergency response teams or military groups, might also benefit from an autocratic leadership style. The capacity to impose discipline and keep order is vital when exact coordination is needed, and there is no space for mistakes. Every team member knows what they're responsible for because of the authoritarian leader's detailed descriptions of their duties, which allows them to work in harmony.

However, to minimize the negative impact of autocratic leadership on team morale and creativity, the leader needs to build relationships with their crew members. Taking the time to understand their strengths, aspirations, and challenges can foster a sense of trust and respect. This personal connection allows the autocratic leader to leverage their crew's talents and capabilities better, maximizing their potential and achieving greater success.

Finally, authoritarian leadership may be effective and strong when used wisely. Autocratic leaders may get their ships aright by learning the ins and outs of this leadership style and mixing it with servant and situational leadership. Autocratic leaders may guide their teams to excellence by keeping morale high, encouraging active participation, and creating an environment where everyone feels comfortable speaking out and sharing ideas. By incorporating elements of servant leadership, autocratic leaders can create a culture of care and support within their teams. This can foster a sense of trust and loyalty, allowing crew members to feel valued and motivated to contribute their best efforts. Additionally, by applying situational leadership, autocratic leaders can adapt their approach to different circumstances, ensuring that decisions are made with appropriate authority and involvement from team members. Ultimately, combining these leadership styles can lead to a harmonious and high-performing crew, resulting in greater success for the entire organization.

3

A Crew of Equals: Democratic Leadership

The Journey:

Imagine yourself standing at the prow of your leadership ship, peering out over its waters with a steady compass that serves as the cornerstone of democratic leadership. But instead of being used as an instrument of absolute authority dictating your path, this magnetic guide always points in a collaborative direction, inviting all hands on deck to help steer it and face whatever storm comes your way together.

Democratic leadership isn't defined by one voice but by a chorus of many voices; it's the art of harmonious collaboration where everyone's talents, ideas, and passions are honored and welcomed as each hand helps steer your ship smoother, uncovers new routes and the journey becomes one written jointly by all participants involved.

Democratic leadership offers many advantages. It fosters creativity by encouraging each team member to provide unique, inventive solutions. Engagement levels remain high as people feel valued and heard while shaping the course of the voyage together. While such idealistic notions may sound idealistic, vessels thrive when diversity coexists with unity.

As our voyage demonstrates, democratic leadership can also present its share of difficult storms. When decisions must be made quickly, waiting for every comment to assemble may take away precious time, sometimes leading to indecision or disagreements. Furthermore, democratic leadership relies heavily on all crew members engaging fully; otherwise, it inevitably falters when participation varies or enthusiasm wanes.

There may be trade-offs; democratic leadership may not work well during times of emergency when quick decisions must be made quickly and without debate. Still, its true potential shines brightest in environments that foster innovation and team collaboration while leaving enough room for dialogue, debate, and consensus-building.

As we embark on our next chapter's journey, remember to use democratic leadership carefully. Recognize its strengths and limitations while knowing when to allow everyone's voices to steer or take the helm yourself and guide. Striking this balance requires deliberate maneuvering, but when done right, everyone on board feels included and together as we ride out democracy together.

Let the journey begin! Democratic leadership sets sail across uncharted waters and navigates uncharted high seas of leadership together. Let's set sail and discover together where democratic leadership thrives, where every voice counts, and where innovation takes root through collective wisdom.

The "What(s)" of Democratic Leadership

The democratic leadership style, often known as participative leadership, is a management style in which the leader encourages the participation of all team members in decision-making processes. Setting it apart from autocratic leadership styles, democratic leaders value consensus and encourage diverse perspectives, fostering an environment of mutual respect, creativity, and commitment among team members.

This leadership style finds its roots in the tenets of democracy, underpinned by principles of freedom, equality, and equitable power distribution. The democratic leader, therefore, does not blindly impose decisions. Instead, they listen, communicate, integrate feedback, and involve their team members in a shared decision-making process.

The democratic leadership style is successful in environments that value innovation and creative problem-solving. Industries encouraging creativity, such as technology, advertising, or academia, are fertile grounds for this leadership style.

We can look at Google's co-founders, Larry Page and Sergey Brin, through an engaging example. Google's famed policy of '20% time' permitted engineers to spend one day a week focusing on an innovative project outside their job description. Many of Google's remarkable products, like Gmail and AdSense, directly resulted from this democratic engagement.

Another example is the late former President of South Africa, Nelson Mandela, who exhibited democratic leadership at a macro level. Despite his tremendous power, Mandela consistently valued shared decision-making, often taking counsel from his team members before making significant decisions. He understood that unilateral decisions without appropriate consultation and buy-in can engender resistance and impede progress.

However, the democratic leadership style is not a panacea for all situations. There could be circumstances where this approach falls short. In crisis or time-sensitive situations, the decision-making process can be slow due to the need for consensus.

A company cannot afford prolonged deliberations during extreme financial or environmental crises. For instance, during the pandemic in 2020, many organizations had to make tough, timely decisions to navigate the crisis successfully. In such scenarios, decisive leadership would be considered more effective than a democratic approach.

Democratic leadership also tends to falter when team members lack sufficient knowledge or experience to contribute effectively to decision-making. In such cases, the guidance and direction of a more autocratic leader is more beneficial. Transitioning into a democratic leader requires conscious effort, patience, and tenacity. The following steps may prove helpful:

An effective democratic leader encourages and requires routine feedback. They regularly solicit team members' input on decisions that directly impact them. Open forums can be an excellent way to encourage participation. They practice active listening skills, pay attention to team members' perspectives, and ensure they feel heard and understood. Effective communication is another cornerstone of democratic leadership. Clear, concise, and consistent communication ensures everyone is on the same page, understanding the 'what' and the 'why' of decisions.

They are empathic and flexible. Effective democratic leaders understand the feelings and perspectives of team members, boost morale, and facilitate better interaction. They are open to change and willing to alter decisions based on feedback or new information.

Remember, democratic leadership is not about diluting one's authority but creating a harmonious balance where power is distributed equitably, decisions are made collaboratively, and every member feels valued and heard.

In the vast ocean of leadership styles, democratic leadership shines like a guiding star, illuminating the pathway to collaboration, inclusivity, and shared decision-making. Imagine a magnificent ship with a talented, diverse crew, each of whom brings a variety of perspectives, experiences, and skills to the table. Democratic leadership harnesses the true potential of this diverse crew, recognizing the immense value that every individual brings and ensuring that each voice is heard, respected, and considered in the pursuit of the voyage's success.

At the core of democratic leadership lies the profound belief that decisions should be made collectively. The leader is not a dictator but a facilitator, creating an environment that encourages active participation and open dialogue among team members. This democratic approach empowers individuals to contribute their ideas, creativity, and expertise, knowing their contributions matter and can significantly impact the ship's direction.

One of the fundamental principles of democratic leadership is the equitable distribution of power. Instead of a hierarchical structure, this leadership style advocates for the sharing and decentralization of power. The leader delegates tasks and responsibilities, allowing team members to take ownership and actively contribute to steering the ship toward its goals. Through this involvement, individuals feel a sense of ownership and agency, fostering a more profound commitment to the collective mission and a desire to excel.

In addition to delegation, the democratic leader assumes the roles of mentor and coach. With a genuine dedication to team members' growth and development, these leaders invest in everyone's success, guiding them to reach their full potential. By providing guidance and support, democratic leaders instill confidence, encourage innovation, and nurture the skills and talents of their crew.

Inherent in effective democratic leadership is the practice of open and transparent communication. Leaders not only convey their ideas and opinions but also actively listen to the perspectives of others. In this safe and inclusive environment, ideas are discussed, challenged, and reined through open dialogue. This collaborative approach leads to better decision-making and fosters camaraderie within the crew, as each member feels heard, valued, and trusted.

Transparency and accountability are essential cornerstones of democratic leadership. Leaders are honest and forthright with their team members, sharing information, providing updates, and ensuring everyone understands the ship's progress and challenges. This transparent approach builds trust and unity within the crew, as they feel an integral part of the decision-making process and the collective journey toward success.

Furthermore, democratic leaders actively seek out and embrace diversity in their crew. They understand that different perspectives and experiences enrich decision-making and promote innovation. These leaders strive to create an environment where individuals from various backgrounds feel welcome and valued, fostering a sense of belonging and empowering each team member to contribute their unique insights.

However, democratic leadership does not imply that all decisions must be made unanimously. While collaborative decision-making is the preferred method, there may be occasions where leaders, leveraging their expertise and experience, must make tough calls. In such cases, democratic leaders explain their rationale and seek input before making a final decision, ensuring every team member feels heard and respected.

More than simply achieving outward success, democratic leadership places immense importance on the growth and development of its crew members. By fostering an environment of respect, empowerment, and collaboration, leaders inspire individuals to go the extra mile, take calculated risks, and contribute their best efforts. This approach drives performance and productivity and cultivates a sense of personal fulfillment and collective achievement.

Democratic leaders also recognize the importance of a continuous learning mindset. They encourage their crew members to seek personal and professional growth opportunities and provide support and resources to facilitate their development. This commitment to lifelong learning ensures that the crew members are equipped with the necessary skills to navigate the ocean's ever-evolving challenges.

As the ship sails forward, the democratic leader understands that the voyage is not solely about reaching a destination but also about nurturing a spirit of togetherness and a sense of collective purpose. By cultivating a crew of equals, democratic leadership establishes fertile ground for collaboration, innovation, and an unwavering commitment to the shared mission. Through their selfless guidance, democratic leaders enable their crew to sail through the challenges of the ocean, transforming an ordinary journey into an extraordinary adventure.

4

Charting the Course: Visionary Leadership

T he Journey:

Once upon a time, in a world filled with people and possibilities, someone dared to gaze toward the future with bright, hopeful eyes—this fascinating character being our visionary leader. Let's set out on a fantastic journey together as we try to comprehend this captivating character and navigate uncharted leadership territory under the guidance of their visionary initiatives.

Imaginative leaders are courageous explorers, adept at perceiving trends and patterns through the telescope of their crystal-clear vision. They dream daringly, striving for what others deem unobtainable. Their strength lies in their ability to inspire, painting vibrant pictures of the future while kindling passion within their team members' hearts so they may transcend ordinary to extraordinary levels.

From such an inspiring tale, one might assume a visionary leader holds an infallible position; however, like our ship navigating turbulent waters, they too possess their weaknesses, one such weakness being their tendency to get so involved with their grand vision that they forget the details or become blindsided by their passion and overlook immediate hurdles—details and assumptions that might eventually prove impediments in their noble quest.

Their passion can often be contagious, yet when taken too far, it may cause discomfort for those who prefer more tranquil and predictable journeys. Furthermore, they can abandon the ship altogether if their lofty ideas don't coincide with an effective implementation plan that ensures their followers remain committed.

Visionary leadership styles excel when innovation is necessary and stagnation needs to be challenged. They also excel in times of turmoil or change and require order from chaos; situations requiring clear direction or psychological uplift also benefit significantly from such leaders.

Visionary leaders may face challenges regarding stability, consistency, and duties that require attention to detail. Their free-flowing ideas might not always work well in contexts that call for pinpoint accuracy. Accompanying our visionary leader on this journey will be an adventure full of hope, difficulty, and eventual reward. With their direction, you can weather any storm and reach your destination with an adventurous spirit, a sense of wonder, and the promise of uncharted territory.

So, let's set sail. Take a deep breath and welcome the wind of change. I anticipate uncharted adventures as we explore the captivating narrative of visionary leadership. A sea of possibilities lies before us, ready to be disrupted and transformed with vision. Come join us on this incredible voyage into visionary leadership's vast ocean!

"What(s)" of Visionary Leadership

As we venture further into the vast waters of leadership, we become mesmerized by its majestic figurehead, the visionary leader. Standing tall against change's gusty winds, this leader becomes more evident as their dreams for an unknown future materialize into tangible plans for a better tomorrow that become crystallized in their eyes - providing guidance and hope along our voyage of exploration.

Visionary leaders inspire us with their visions, acting like navigators of uncharted oceans. Their insights, stirring speeches, and progressive mentalities steer organizations toward promising horizons, almost like their leaders possess an internal compass guiding them away from status quo territories toward lusher pastures. As we sail along with the Visionary Leader, we see other vessels in the distance with individual leaders at their helms - let's take a closer look at these ships and their captains!

Leadership is a vast expanse, like the overwhelming diversity of the sea. Exploring it requires fortitude, wisdom, and strategy. Here, we dive deep into the waters of visionary leadership, comparing its currents with other significant styles like autocratic, democratic, servant, transformative, why-based, and purposeful leadership. This investigation enables us to understand better how these styles interact, overlap, and contrast.

Visionary leadership acts as the compass that guides an organization toward its future. It defines the direction of the journey, motivates the crew, and consistently communicates the organization's purpose—the cardinal "why." However, this commanding gaze into the horizon has its challenges. The visionary leader's grand designs may overlook immediate operational quirks, potentially unsettling the crew or causing resource misallocation. The scenario is particularly crucial when coping with sudden storms or organizational crises, where more autocratic or democratic leadership styles may prove beneficial. Autocratically-led vessels anchored firmly in their home waters feature gallant vessels led by autocratic leaders. While our visionary leaders rule with gentle care and discretion, the autocrats rule with a firm hand; their ship travels the meticulously charted waters under strict orders, with efficiency and discipline being their hallmarks of excellence. Autocratic leaders can swiftly respond to crises, their strong unilateral decisions navigating through the storm, while democratic leaders intelligently leverage collective wisdom.

Comparatively, servant leaders prioritize the crew's welfare, ensuring their needs are met, enhancing morale, and fostering loyalty—essential factors in long-term journeys. Still, more than these bonds might be needed to chart a clear path forward, necessitating the visionary's "visionary" foresight.

Transformative leaders, the shapeshifters of the sea, take elements from each style as needed, adeptly pivoting to meet the changing environment. Their flexibility can thrive in any situation, though without a clear, consistent "why," it can lead to confusion and loss of purpose.

Why-based and purposeful leadership responds to this need by providing a clear reason and purpose, a shared aspect of the visionary style. They maintain a strong connection with the "why," but where the visionary style dreams big and maps the course, these styles focus on the 'how' and 'what.' Yet, their purpose-driven approach is directed toward immediate tasks, needing more horizon-gaze of the visionary leader.

The most fertile ground for visionary leadership lies within a culture fostering freedom of ideas, paired with the disciplined implementation of such ideas. An organization that is open to change, oriented towards learning, and empowers individuals to contribute beyond their assigned roles echoes the visionary leader's call to arms. It necessitates strategic alignment, cascading clear communication channels, and ensuring everyone understands how their roles contribute to realizing the shared vision, thus making the "why" a vital part of their work routine.

On a more representative current, we find the democratic leader. Their strength lies in harnessing the collective abilities of their crew, engaging every sailor in decision-making processes while instilling an atmosphere of responsibility and dedication across the board. Democratic leaders eager to immerse themselves in the visionary style must embrace risk-taking decisiveness, foster creativity, communicate compelling visions, and, most importantly, stay committed to nurturing the "why" in their organizations.

Our roadmap to developing visionary leadership includes understanding other styles and valuing their strengths, becoming proficient at change management, honing communication skills, weaving the "why" into the organization's fabric, and perpetual self-reflection coupled with feedback from the crew.

To become more effective visionary leaders, it may be helpful to regularly assess critical areas for improvement, engage in leadership workshops focusing on long-term strategic planning, and seek mentorship from successful visionary leaders.

Remember, leadership is not a destination but a continuous journey. Despite the challenges, the call of visionary leadership echoes steadily amidst the waves, spawning fresh lands of opportunity. The visionary leader's mantra is the significant "why," piercing the fog of uncertainty, rallying the crew, propelling the vessel towards unseen horizons, and captivating the hearts and minds of every voyager on board.

At sea, another ship glimmers radiantly under its transformational leader's leadership. Its leaders possess many of the same traits as our visionary leaders, such as rallying their crew behind a shared vision yet surpassing them by actively changing, improving, and challenging them to grow alongside the organization and transform themselves.

At last, a ship sails with purposeful navigation led by its why-based or purposeful leader. Their purposeful mantra echoes our visionary's "vision" as they both focus on driving their vessels with 'why.' While our visionary leader looks toward the future for inspiration and guidance, purposeful leaders continually refer to their organization's deep-seated purpose to steer their vessel toward this 'why.'

As our understanding of these remarkable figures deepens, we appreciate leadership's multi-dimensional aspects. Visionary leaders stand out against other leadership styles, each providing its own perspective on how to perceive and navigate this ever-evolving field of leadership.

Utilizing our telescope of exploration, we continue our voyage of discovering effective leadership. Through its many faces and forms, leadership shapes the course of organizations. Join us as we unravel its many threads through each chapter as we navigate the complex waters that make up leadership theory.

Visionary leaders stand out by their unique ability to inspire their teams with an inspiring vision of the future, delineating its path, infusing passion and optimism, and stimulating intellectual potential within their teams. Such leaders possess an uncanny knack for identifying future trends while possessing exceptional foresight to predict and overcome future challenges, taking their organizations into new territories. At the same time, their gaze remains focused on their lofty aims, while their feet stay firmly grounded in their daily actions toward their lofty aims.

Visionary leadership stands apart from other variants of

leadership, such as autocratic, democratic, servant-leadership, transformational, or purposeful, in that its characteristics differ significantly while sharing some similarities. By placing visionary leadership next to these other leadership models, we see significant variations and overlaps emerge.

Autocratic leadership, which relies on central decision-making, starkly contrasts with visionary leadership. Where autocrats often dictate decisions without consulting followers or encouraging a culture of intellectual stimulation and innovation, visionary leaders involve followers in decision-making while still providing clear direction. Both have decisiveness and clarity for followers in common.

Democratic leadership emphasizes equal-opportunity decision-making processes and can differ significantly from visionary and autocratic styles. Democratic leaders rely more on group consensus when making decisions; visionary leaders, however, provide clear direction regarding decision-making processes.

With its "we-before-me" philosophy, servant leadership shares many commonalities with visionary leadership. Both approaches are interested in people's needs and personal development; however, servant leaders focus more on empowering and elevating followers, while visionary leaders focus on realizing the vision. Servant leaders take a different approach: serving their crew members instead of leading from behind the wheel. Their actions stem not from ambition but genuine care for their members, believing that a happy, productive crew will naturally navigate to prosperous shores.

Transformative leadership aims for radical transformation within organizations. Both types of leaders use followers' intellectual resources and encourage creativity; however, transformational leaders typically drive change within an existing setup, while visionary leaders create an overall future state vision.

Purposeful and "why"-based leadership theories also overlap with visionary leadership theories, providing compelling reasons for engagement to spark intrinsic motivation. While both 'why"-based and visionary leadership techniques emphasize creating a shared understanding of an organization's purpose and envisioning its realization into vivid future states, purposeful leadership emphasizes engagement and commitment towards meaningful missions instead of creating specific visions.

Overall, leadership styles can be complex. Successful leaders often employ multiple styles, including visionary approaches, depending on the situational context and followers' needs. An effective form of leadership does not need to be rigid and inflexible; instead, it should adapt to different teams across various situations to bring out the best performance from teams. Our next chapter covers this in more depth.

Visionary leadership is integral to success in the vast ocean of leadership styles. Visionary leaders possess a unique ability to envision a future that has yet to be realized and chart a course toward that vision with unwavering determination and conviction.

At the heart of visionary leadership is the leader's capacity to see beyond the confines of the present and imagine possibilities that others may overlook. They possess the foresight to anticipate trends, changes, and disruptions in their industry or organization. By meticulously analyzing data and information, they interpret signals from the market and society. This enables them to connect seemingly unrelated dots and construct a comprehensive picture of the future.

The visionary leader's creative mindset allows them to imagine innovative solutions to emerging challenges. They understand that conventional approaches often fail to adapt to an ever-changing world. Therefore, they encourage experimentation and foster a culture of innovation within their team or organization. Challenging established norms and embracing calculated risks inspire their team members to think outside the box and explore new avenues. They understand that breakthroughs often occur at the intersection of diverse ideas and perspectives and thus actively seek out input from different voices within their team.

Effective communication of the vision is a hallmark characteristic of visionary leaders. They are skilled storytellers with a remarkable ability to paint a vivid picture of the desired future. Through compelling narratives, visuals, and metaphors, they bring their vision to life, igniting the imagination of their team members. By illustrating the benefits and opportunities that lie ahead, they create an emotional connection with their audience, inspiring them to rally behind the vision. Moreover, visionary leaders understand the importance of aligning the vision with the core values and purpose of the organization,

53

making it a source of inspiration and motivation for the entire team.

However, a vision without a roadmap is merely a dream. A visionary leader diligently breaks down their vision into tangible goals and actionable steps. By collaborating with their team, they create a strategic plan that outlines the necessary milestones and timelines for achieving the vision. This roadmap provides their team members with clarity and direction, ensuring everyone is aligned and focused on the goal. Additionally, the roadmap is a tool to measure progress and make necessary adjustments.

While visionary leaders have a clear vision and plan, they also recognize that the path to the envisioned future is rarely linear. They understand the importance of adaptability and resilience in facing unforeseen circumstances. Like skilled navigators, they remain agile and adjust their course when needed. They anticipate and leverage change, transforming potential obstacles into opportunities for growth and innovation. They encourage their team to embrace ambiguity and learn from failures, recognizing they are essential stepping stones toward progress.

Empowering and delegating are crucial aspects of visionary leadership. A visionary leader understands the value of assembling a team of talented individuals with complementary skills and expertise. They believe in creating an environment that nurtures collaboration, trust, and shared accountability. By empowering their team members to take ownership of their work, make decisions, and contribute their unique perspectives, the visionary leader harnesses the collective intelligence and creativity of the entire organization. They can identify and develop the potential within each team member, fostering a sense of empowerment and growth within the team.

The visionary leader actively seeks feedback and cultivates a culture of open communication. They understand that collective wisdom is invariably more powerful than individual insights. They encourage their team members to share their opinions, ideas, and concerns, fostering an inclusive and psychologically safe environment where every voice is valued and respected. Through effective communication and active listening, they create platforms for dialogue that encourage diverse perspectives, leading to more innovative and well-rounded solutions.

In summary, visionary leadership is a multi-dimensional approach that requires seeing beyond the present, communicating effectively, adapting to change, empowering others, and fostering a culture of collaboration and innovation. A visionary leader navigates through uncharted waters, inspiring and motivating their team to embrace the shared vision and charting a course that leads to success and greatness. Through their transformative leadership, they shape the future of their organization and leave a lasting impact on the world.

5

Rising with the Tide: Transformative Leadership

The Journey:

Imagine it's dawn, with an air of delicate crispness and the sun dancing across the horizon; you are standing on top of a hill gazing down at an endless path below, with each step marking another journey into yourself and change—an expedition into transformative leadership itself!

Transformative leadership evokes images of profound transformation, significant transition, and great potential, which it does encapsulate. But transformative leadership goes further: it involves something deeper: inspiring people not by exerting authority but instead awakening their sense of purpose and potential.

As we travel down this path of transformative leadership, we encounter its inherent strength: its capacity to match group ambitions with a leader's vision. But this goes beyond simply having a dream—it means making that dream tangible so it becomes something others can see, embrace, and work towards together. That is the true magic of transformative leaders— they don't simply instruct a course of action but instead stir souls by inspiring people to become their best selves.

However, while leading transformative change may appear alluring and exciting, it is challenging. Like any worthwhile journey, leading transformative change requires facing off against complex terrain—often making difficult, unpopular decisions with severe ramifications for personal and professional relationships.

Transformative leadership may only sometimes be the optimal approach; during times of crisis or when immediate action is necessary, transformative leadership may seem cumbersome as its work primarily relies on gradual changes toward collective goals. Furthermore, organizations with deeply entrenched cultures may struggle with change as resistance may arise within these walls.

However, remember that every journey, ambition, or transformation starts with one step. So let's embark on our own exploration if we are ready for its trials, uncertainties, and ultimate wide-eyed wonder of discovery. Let's find transformative leadership not as scientists peering through microscopes but as travelers searching to understand human emotions at work within an atmosphere of ambition, resilience, and purpose.

Welcome, adventurer. Let's embark upon our voyage through transformative leadership, where change's waves hold out the promise of new horizons.

As we progress through this chapter, we will develop a more detailed picture of transformative leadership journeys- both its allure and challenges.

"What(s)" of Transformative Leadership

At the heart of transformative change lie leaders who inspire, challenge, and empower others with their vision, evoking significant personal and professional growth. This chapter will explore the dimensions of transformational leadership style, its implications within diverse contexts, real-life examples, and a roadmap for developing this vital leadership competency.

Transformational leadership is a style that, in essence, is about inspiring followers to transcend their self-interests for the collective good of the organization. It involves leaders engendering change and advancement to their staff through inspiration enthusiasm, and stimulating a sense of commit-ment and shared vision.

The concept emanates from the work of James V. Downton, later developed extensively by James Burns and Bernard M. Bass. Burns (1978) distinguished transactional leaders (who engage in a 'transaction' or exchange process with their followers) from transformational leaders, framing the latter as individuals who encourage followers to exceed individual performance expectations.

58

Transformational leadership operates on four fundamental facets: intellectual stimulation, individualized consideration, inspirational motivation, and idealized influence ('The Four I's').

Intellectual Stimulation: Leaders challenge their team members' thinking and creativity, promoting innovation and problem-solving skills.

Individualized Consideration: Transformational leaders foster an environment that recognizes and nurtures individual talents, making team members feel valued and motivated.

Inspirational Motivation: Leaders articulate a clear, attractive, and inspiring future state that encourages followers to buy into the shared vision.

Idealized Influence: Transformational leaders act as role models, maintaining high ethical and moral standards that build trust and respect.

When employed adeptly, transformational leadership can profoundly affect satisfaction, efficiency, and overall productivity within the organizational setting.

Where does transformational leadership function best, and where may it fall short? Despite its potential, transformational leadership has its drawbacks. This style can be seen as overbearing, cult-like, or manipulative in some contexts, specifically if the leader strays from ethical guidelines. Some leaders may need to be more comfortable with their level of charisma or personal development focus.

Moreover, transformational leaders might need to emphasize big-picture thinking and vision, neglecting vital details and operational concerns. They also unrealistically amplify followers' expectations, creating disappointment and disillusionment.

Lastly, since transformational leadership heavily relies on the leader's charisma and influence, the absence of such a leader might create a leadership vacuum, causing instability in the organization.

Over the years, many "captains" have embodied the transformational leader. Historically, figures such as Nelson Mandela and Martin Luther King Jr., who envisioned radical societal transformations and infused their followers with a sense of shared purpose, embody transformational leadership styles.

In the business world, Richard Branson, Founder of Virgin Group, exhibits transformational leadership traits by promoting an entrepreneurial culture within his companies, empowering employees, and inspiring them with his bold visions.

How would a leader go about developing and enhancing these specific traits? Developing transformational leadership skills involves cultivating interpersonal competencies and self-awareness. A potential leader should start by fostering a compelling vision and articulating this vision clearly and convincingly to engage followers.

Leaders should also invest time understanding their team members more profoundly and recognizing their aspirations, strengths, and developmental needs. This could be achieved through coaching and mentoring.

Instilling a culture of innovation and intellectual curiosity is another crucial aspect. Leaders create safe environments for teams to voice out-of-the-box ideas and challenge the status quo.

Lastly, consistency in personal behavior is integral to the transformational leadership style, which ultimately establishes the leader as a role model. This requires maintaining high ethical and moral standards and demonstrating behaviors that align with the organization's values and vision.

Transformational leadership offers more than a means of managing, directing, or inspiring; it encompasses a holistic approach to reshaping individual and organizational futures. By understanding its dynamics, appreciating its merits and demerits, and adapting its tenets, leaders can harness the power of transformational leadership to inspire significant and worthwhile change within their professional sphere.

Transformative leadership is an ongoing process where leaders and followers collaborate to increase morale and motivation among members of both groups. Transformative leaders provide their followers with inspiration and motivation that goes beyond what is typically expected, encouraging creative thinking while exerting maximum effort, leading them to greater innovation, creativity, and exceptional results than otherwise.

How does the transformative location on our map compare to our other stops along our journey? In stark contrast to transformative leadership, autocratic leaders make decisions without consulting their teams, often feeling that their decision is final and unchallenged. Although autocratic leaders may successfully manage teams and resolve issues promptly, this type of leadership often needs to be improved where creativity, out-of-the-box thinking, and individual morale contribute towards group or organizational success. Autocratic leaders can help complete tasks more quickly with no disruptions due to autonomy, whereas transformative leaders foster innovation while building employee morale over the long term.

Democratic leadership entails delegating decision-making authority to team members while taking overall responsibility for their success as an organization. Democratic leadership is considered one of the most effective leadership styles as it allows shared decision-making and encourages creativity; however, this approach may result in slower decision-making during times of crisis and less efficiency overall than transformative leaders who provide inspiration and motivation with specific direction and purpose.

Visionary and transformative leadership share many similarities; both styles aim to inspire and motivate team members to reach their full potential. They differ in approach: visionary leaders articulate an ideal future that they can persuade their followers to embrace; in contrast, transformative leaders have a vision but focus more on challenging beliefs, values, and attitudes and encouraging innovation and creativity among team members.

Servant leadership differs from transformative leadership in that it mainly emphasizes facilitating team members' growth and well-being rather than inspiring personal or professional advancement for themselves or pursuing a shared vision. While servant leaders put people's needs before their own and try to help their teams perform optimally, transformative leaders tend to inspire followers through personal or professional growth while leading toward shared visions.

Purposeful (or why-based) leadership rests on the belief that people are motivated not by tasks themselves but by why they must be done (the purpose behind each task). While transformative leaders tend to motivate followers by challenging them to go beyond self-interest for the greater good of their team or organization, purposeful leaders achieve this effect by aligning tasks with their followers' sense of purpose or passion.

Transformational leadership is an engaging and multilayered form of leadership that inspires followers to accomplish more than they ever believed possible, cultivating an atmosphere of innovation, creativity, and broad-based engagement. While having similarities and distinctions from autocratic, democratic, visionary, servant, and purposeful leadership models, it remains unique in its capacity to drive personal and organizational development.

In the vast ocean of leadership styles, transformative leadership stands tall as a beacon of change and growth. Transformative leaders possess the unique ability to inspire and motivate their teams to reach new heights while simultaneously fostering personal and organizational transformation.

One key characteristic of transformative leadership is the emphasis on individual development. Transformative leaders understand that true change begins from within and stems from understanding oneself. They believe that by helping their team members realize their full potential, they can create a ripple effect that reaches far beyond the confines of the organization. This dedication to personal growth not only enhances the skills and capabilities of individuals but also cultivates a sense of empowerment and motivation to pursue excellence.

Transformative leaders invest in mentorship and coaching to facilitate their team members' growth. Recognizing that guidance and support can be pivotal in shaping one's journey, they actively seek opportunities to provide valuable insights and advice. By acting as trusted mentors, they foster an environment of learning, enabling their team members to overcome obstacles, develop new skills, and ultimately become leaders.

However, the mentorship relationship is not one-sided. Transformative leaders understand the value of reverse mentoring, where they learn from their team members; they recognize the wealth of knowledge and fresh perspectives that can be gained by actively engaging in conversations and seeking input from individuals at all levels of the organization. This allows for a continuous exchange of ideas and ensures that the leader remains open-minded and adaptable to new ways of thinking.

Additionally, transformative leaders recognize the importance of self-awareness. They understand that leading others effectively starts with deeply understanding their strengths, weaknesses, and values. Through introspection and reflective practices, they gain insight into their leadership style and its impact on others. This self-awareness enables them to lead authentically, showcasing their genuine selves and allowing their team members to connect with them on a deeper level.

Furthermore, transformative leaders understand the power of emotional intelligence. They are attuned to the emotions and needs of their team members, creating a supportive and empathetic environment. They foster trust and build stronger relationships with their team members by demonstrating empathy, active listening, and compassion. This emotional connection forms the foundation for collaboration and encourages a sense of psychological safety, where individuals feel comfortable expressing their ideas, thoughts, and concerns.

A transformative leader also creates a compelling vision that transcends the status quo. They are skilled at articulating a clear, inspiring purpose that resonates with their team members. They create a shared purpose and direction by aligning individual goals with the overarching vision. This shared vision becomes a rallying point, empowering team members to go above and beyond their perceived limitations and work collectively towards a common goal.

However, inspiring a shared vision is more than just about

the leader's communication skills. Transformative leaders understand the importance of active involvement and co-creation. They engage their team members in the vision-setting process, encouraging them to contribute their ideas and insights. By empowering individuals to have a stake in defining the path ahead, transformative leaders increase ownership, commitment, and accountability across the organization.

Building upon the foundation of trust, transformative leaders promote a culture of open and transparent communication. They foster an environment where everyone's voice is valued and encouraged and where diverse perspectives are sought and respected. Through regular and authentic conversations, they create opportunities for dialogue, feedback, and dissent. This open communication strengthens teamwork and collaboration and enables the generation of innovative ideas and solutions.

Transformative leaders also understand the importance of celebrating successes and milestones along the journey. They recognize that acknowledgment and recognition are pivotal in boosting morale, fostering a positive work environment, and reinforcing the commitment to an individual's growth and development. By appreciating their team members' collective efforts and achievements, transformative leaders create a culture of appreciation and motivation.

In addition, transformative leaders embrace risk-taking and encourage innovation. They understand that transformative change requires breaking traditional norms and exploring new possibilities. Creating a safe space for experimentation and learning from failure inspires their team members to take calculated risks, challenge the status quo, and think outside the box. This openness to embracing uncertainty and failure as a stepping stone toward success drives continuous improvement and fuels organizational innovation.

Furthermore, transformative leaders are advocates for adaptability and resilience. They understand that we live in a dynamic and rapidly evolving world where staying relevant requires adapting quickly to change. These leaders cultivate a growth mindset within their teams, encouraging a continuous learning and development mindset. They foster a culture of resilience, where setbacks and challenges are viewed as opportunities for growth and learning. By embracing change and addressing adversity head-on, transformative leaders navigate their teams through times of uncertainty and empower individuals to thrive amidst complexities and ambiguity.

Last but not least, transformative leaders strive to leave a lasting impression and have a profound purpose. They understand that leadership is about achieving short-term goals and creating a legacy built on meaning and significance. They strive to make a difference in the lives of their team members, the organization, and the world. Through their leadership, they inspire their teams to become engaged citizens, encouraging them to contribute positively to their communities and tackle complex societal issues.

In conclusion, transformative leadership goes beyond merely managing teams and tasks. It is about creating a culture of growth, empowering individuals, and driving meaningful change. Transformative leaders invest in individual development, foster strong relationships, communicate transparently, inspire a shared vision, encourage risk-taking and innovation, embrace adaptability, and lead with a profound purpose. By embodying these qualities, transformative leaders empower their teams to rise with the tide of change and create a lasting impact on the world.

6

Putting the Crew First: Servant Leadership

J ourney

As our voyage continues, our journey continues onboard the tall ship "SS Leadership," an old vessel that has seen more than its share of stormy seas and turbulent weather. Captain Elara embodies servant leadership—wind in her hair, salt air on her lips, and a sparkle in her eyes that extends far beyond the horizon. What sets Captain Elara apart from others in leadership circles is not her skill or bravery in facing storms but her natural ability to serve her crew even while leading them.

Servant leaders like Captain Elara prioritize the needs of their crew over their own. No matter whether the team is mired in doldrums or bracing itself for the storm, Elara always rises first to ensure her people's spirits remain undamaged, their bellies full, and skills developed, seeing herself not simply as an aesthetic figurehead but as the one providing vital guidance and direction.

Sailing legend describes numerous qualities of an ideal captain, which align neatly with servant leaders' expectations. Elara stands out as an embodiment of these virtues in both humility and learning orientation—never afraid to learn something new and seek feedback—knowing that the growth of her ship and herself go hand-in-hand. In times of severe storms or gentle calm, Elara displays empathy towards her crew, keeping an eye out for their morale or challenges while inspiring them with stories of new places they'll soon reach. Finally, there is courage—having the strength to make difficult choices while taking responsibility for her decisions, failures, and achievements despite her challenges.

Becoming a servant leader, like our esteemed captain, isn't something one does overnight; it is a long journey, often against the current. Cultivating empathy requires listening without prejudice and understanding different viewpoints; developing humility requires accepting lifelong learning with unbiased feedback; earning and maintaining trust involves being consistently honest and transparent in actions taken; simply put, a steadfast commitment to personal development and people-centric values is what directs prospective servant leaders towards their destination.

The undulating waves of the ocean parallel the unpredictable rhythms of the corporate world, where servant leadership thrives in environments characterized by collaboration, in-

PUTTING THE CREW FIRST: SERVANT LEADERSHIP

novation, and long-term growth. When storm clouds loom on their horizon, Elara takes charge and forms a collective approach to dealing with impending obstacles by gathering her crew for discussion sessions that encourage ideas while considering all perspectives.

However, in situations that demand quick decisions—when stormy seas hit and there is no time for democratic deliberation of ideas—classical servant leadership might prove suboptimal. Delaying actions may prove too long-winded; more authoritative leadership styles might be necessary instead to steer away from hazardous reefs. Furthermore, the sudden implementation of servant leadership might create confusion among crew members already entrenched in strict hierarchical norms; its sudden implementation could cause chaos that threatens to capsize the ship without careful management.

Servant leadership, like Siren's song, isn't meant for every sailor; it's meant for those drawn to its principles: service over individual glory and collective success over individual fame. Carrying its flag requires constant tending of virtues: when to engage participative democracy versus drop the anchor of command; Captain Elara continues her voyage across the vast sea, exemplifying servant leadership while leaving an everlasting mark that will long be remembered in the ocean's depths.

With dawn breaking on the horizon and ocean waves lapping upon its shores, gentle whispers resonated. Soon enough, you find yourself aboard an elegant ship, its timbers shining with sunlight. Our journey now turns toward less traveled roads;

with salty sea air caressing us gently, we set sail toward servant leadership.

Servant leadership is an odyssey of profound personal change. An unsaid desire to make a positive contribution or the niggling whisper of calling often initiates the transition into selflessness. Servant leaders lead with empathy, humility, and respect as their priorities and place others' needs before their own.

Servant leadership promises strengthened bonds, elevated morale, employee development, and enhanced team performance as we gaze upon its strengths. A humble captain who inspires her crew towards an organic mission rather than barking orders follows servant leadership practices, not barking orders as per traditional methods but leading through garnering trust, fostering collaboration, and empowering others.

Servant leadership can be turbulent. Amid its waves lie its vulnerabilities: decisions may become slow due to the need for consensus, power dynamics may become unclear, and leaders may become subservient, prioritizing others' needs over strategic objectives. There may also be a risk that leaders are exploited due to being too empathic, leading to potential team conflict, miscommunication, or reductions in efficiency and productivity.

This chapter will serve as your navigation system in these waters, like an ancient mariner using a map for guidance. The servant leadership approach thrives within organizations focused on purpose and hungering for authentic community, those interested in distributed decision-making, integrative thinkers who value personal development equally to objectives or profits, and individuals looking for ethical yet compassionate conflict resolution strategies.

However, this model may require more work to attain decisiveness, clear power boundaries, and swift action. Servant leadership could prove unsuitable for highly competitive environments or situations where quick, authoritative decisions must be made quickly and decisively. However, as we explore this method further, we realize it extends far beyond an organization and affects every aspect of life.

Now, as our ship plunges into a turbulent sea tossed by fierce winds, its sails billow out with the promise of servant leadership driven by an entirely different compass. As we explore this captivating leadership style further, your perspective may forever change—servant leadership may soon emerge into the light! Are you willing to embrace its light?

"What(s)" of Servant Leadership

As we explore servant leadership further, its contours become clearer. Servant leaders strive to serve others sincerely while supporting their growth; these individuals share power freely while placing people above roles; they are empathic, have great foresight, and foster team prosperity as part of a continuous personal development cycle that enhances team success as much as personal success does.

Servant leadership, a term coined by Robert K. Greenleaf in

1970, represents a holistic approach to leadership. In this style, leaders prioritize the needs and development of their team members above their own, cultivating an environment where subordinates feel valued, appreciated, and supported to realize their full potential. Servant leaders operate on the principle that when they serve their team members with selflessness and humility, the natural corollary will foster stronger, more productive collaborations, increased morale, and better organizational performance.

Where Servant Leadership Flourishes

Servant Leadership is specifically viable in mission-driven organizations, non-profit entities, and industries emphasizing employee well-being and participation. Consider the case of Starbucks, where the CEO Howard Schultz adopted servant leadership principles as organizational values. His focus on the welfare of employees, provision of comprehensive benefits, and consistent emphasis on ethical standards bolstered employee loyalty, fostering a culture that contributed to the brand's global success.

The Mayo Clinic, a world-renowned healthcare organization, is another testament to servant leadership. Clinicians and administrators are enshrined in a culture of serving patients' needs above all else, culminating in excellent patient satisfaction ratings and a reputation for high-quality patient care.

Where does it fall short? Despite its appeal, servant leadership may not always be the panacea for all organizations. This leadership style might be challenging in highly competitive sectors where results-driven performances are paramount. Focusing excessively on employees' well-being might de-emphasize goal attainment and competitive edge in such contexts.

Furthermore, in large organizations, the extensive personal attention and deep emotional investment required by servant leaders may not be feasible, given the sheer size and complexity of the established hierarchies.

A third limitation pertains to potential followers' exploitation. A servant leader's selflessness might be misinterpreted as a weakness, leading to opportunism by less scrupulous team members.

Despite these constraints, individuals can develop servant leadership skills. It begins with a genuine interest in other people's well-being and a desire to support their growth.

Emotional intelligence, an essential ingredient of this leader-ship style, is pivotal for leaders to manage their emotions when relating to their team members. Leaders need to develop their empathy and active listening skills to understand and address the needs of their team. Leonard Cheshire, an international disability charity, for instance, offers training to its employees to enhance these skills, leading to improved workplace well-being and productivity.

Communication skills must be honed for clear, concise, and constructive discourse. This will empower team members and clarify organizational goals, responsibilities, and how they fit into the larger picture.

Finally, leaders should be adaptable, understanding that different situations may require different leadership styles. They need to strike a balance between their nurturing inclinations as servant leaders and the objective needs of their organization.

As we continue our journey through servant leadership, we can read our map by comparing and contrasting this method with other destinations on our quest. We contrast servant leadership with autocratic leadership, which can be likened to an admiral leading a fleet into combat. Under such leadership, their orders cannot be questioned, and decisions made essentially dictate the path forward; rewards or punishment are issued according to compliance or rebellion, respectively. Although autocratic leadership may drive rapid results in high-stakes situations, servant leaders empower, encourage, and foster mutual respect and growth among their teams.

Democrats favor democratic leadership, treating their position like a wise council leader by welcoming feedback, stimulating conversations, and making decisions with group input. Servant leadership also uses democratic principles as its core; the distinction lies in intent; while both recognize people's voices equally highly, democratic leaders utilize collective wisdom primarily for decision-making, while servant leaders focus on serving team development and needs more actively than their democratic counterparts.

Visionary leadership allows leaders to act as farsighted navigators, offering compelling images of the desired destination and leaving room for individual creativity. While visionary and servant leadership share many similarities in inspiring and encouraging their employees, their primary thrusts differ considerably: one offers an inspiring vision while the latter guides through subtle currents of empathy and service.

Navigating toward transformative leadership reveals leaders like an astute captain navigating stormy seas of change for their ship's progress. Transformative and servant leaders thrive in dynamic environments and empower others through inspiration and intellectual stimulation. Both types of leaders strive towards individual and organizational growth; transformative leaders focus on raising performance levels through change, while servant leaders prioritize meeting followers' needs, which can foster increased performance levels.

Purposeful leadership stands as an oasis in an otherwise aimless landscape. These leaders embrace purpose as their guiding compass; similar qualities exist between this type and servant leadership, yet the latter's emphasis on the well-being of team members and service to others differentiates it.

In summary, servant leadership can, under the appropriate conditions, prove to be a transformative leadership style. At its core, it prioritizes individuals, forging more profound connections between leaders and their teams and facilitating a harmonious, productive work environment. This approach can yield remarkable organizational achievements when balanced with vigilance about potential pitfalls.

After our voyage, we encountered the many-faceted nature of

leadership. Each style holds value in various environments. Servant leadership's commitment to humane and empathetic behavior often proves invaluable when working in environments that foster trust, autonomy, and purposeful endeavors. As we navigate this ocean of leadership knowledge, the gentle light of servant leadership will illuminate us all while we discover its practical applications and benefits.

Servant leadership emerges as a refreshing and transformative alternative in a world where leadership is often associated with power, authority, and control. It is a leadership style that requires individuals to forsake self-interest and prioritize the needs, growth, and well-being of others above all else. Rather than using their position of authority to exert dominance or achieve personal gain, servant leaders selflessly serve those they lead.

Servant leadership is deeply rooted in the idea that leaders should be in service to their followers, guiding and supporting them to reach their full potential. This leadership philosophy, first put forth by Robert K. Greenleaf in the 1970s, has gained popularity in recent years as an alternative to conventional top-down leadership models. It fosters a culture of collaboration, empathy, and trust, enabling individuals and teams to thrive.

At the core of servant leadership is actively listening to others. Servant leaders understand the importance of listening to their team members and genuinely seeking to understand their perspectives, needs, and aspirations. They listen not only with their ears but also with their hearts, demonstrating empathy and a genuine interest in others. By doing so, they create an environment where everyone feels heard and valued. This authentic engagement improves relationships and communication and leads to increased engagement and commitment from team members.

Putting others first also means prioritizing the growth and development of individuals within the team. Servant leaders invest time and effort in nurturing their followers' skills and talents, providing them opportunities to learn, grow, and take on new challenges.

They act as mentors, coaches, and advocates, empowering their team members to reach their full potential. By fostering a continuous learning and development culture, servant leaders enable their teams to adapt to ever-changing circumstances and contribute effectively to the organization's success.

In addition to personal development, servant leaders are committed to the holistic well-being of their team members. They recognize that individuals bring their whole selves to work with unique personal and professional challenges. Servant leaders take a genuine interest in the lives of their followers, providing support, flexibility, and understanding during difficult times. They prioritize work-life balance, mental health initiatives, and initiatives that promote physical wellness. Such leaders understand this by caring for their team members. As individuals, they create an environment where everyone can thrive and flourish.

One essential aspect of servant leadership is the willingness to make personal sacrifices for the team's greater good. Servant leaders understand that their role is not about personal gain but about serving the collective goals and needs of the organization. This may involve making tough decisions, taking responsibility for failures, and actively supporting the success of others, even if it means stepping back or letting others take the spotlight. By placing the interests of others above their own, servant leaders create loyalty, trust, and a sense of purpose within the team.

Servant leaders also recognize the importance of building positive relationships based on trust and respect. They foster an inclusive and supportive environment where everyone feels safe to express their ideas, concerns, and opinions. This open communication and collaboration create a sense of belonging and shared purpose within the team. Moreover, servant leaders are approachable, displaying empathy and emotional intelligence, which allows them to connect with individuals on a deeper level and build strong bonds of trust.

Furthermore, servant leaders lead by example. They embody the values and behaviors they wish to see in others, inspiring their team members to follow suit. By consistently demonstrating integrity, humility, and a commitment to ethical practices, they set the tone for a culture of servant leadership throughout the organization. They actively engage in servant leadership practices, such as empowering others, facilitating collaboration, and fostering a sense of community.

Servant leadership goes beyond superficial gestures and requires a deep understanding and appreciation of others' diverse needs, experiences, and perspectives. It challenges leaders to examine their biases and prejudices to create an inclusive and equitable environment that celebrates diversity. Servant leaders actively seek out the voices often marginalized or silenced and work towards empowering them to thrive.

Servant leadership is a powerful and transformative approach that centers around putting others first. It involves actively listening, nurturing growth, supporting well-being, making personal sacrifices, building trust, and leading by example. By embracing this leadership style, individuals can create a positive and empowering environment that brings out the best in others and drives collective success. Servant leadership is not a sign of weakness but a demonstration of strength, empathy, and an unwavering commitment to serving others. It is a call to leaders to step away from self-centeredness and embrace the profound impact they can have by putting others at the forefront of their leadership journey.

7

Charting our Purpose: Why-Based Leadership

T he Journey:

As we embark on our leadership voyage together, imagine standing on a harbor edge, gazing out across an infinite sea. Seagulls call overhead while the sea breeze whispers around you, evoking excitement within. An ancient and well-worn map charting your course and a reliable compass guiding your every move is at your side. Courage pulses steadily in your heart—this compass and ocean symbolize our next leg: Why-Based Leadership.

As with a compass, why-based leadership provides direction by giving leaders a clear sense of purpose and meaning behind all actions, decisions, and strategies. Why-based leadership serves as the ultimate compass in an organization, providing its true north, driving purpose, and an overall roadmap of its journey.

Why-based leadership boasts many advantages. At its core is a fantastic sense of team unity created by aligned goals, which leads to increased team performance and commitment. Why-based leaders create an atmosphere where employees feel validated and appreciated while understanding their role within a bigger picture. They inspire followers beyond self-interested goals toward organizational ones while aligning personal ones with organizational ones for maximum employee dedication and advocacy.

However, why-based leadership can present its own set of unique challenges. At times, its compelling appeal may cause leaders to lose sight of how or what to accomplish, leading them down an ineffective path or shifting priorities improperly. Furthermore, maintaining relevance without diluting its essence requires constant reaffirmation and adjustment as circumstances shift, which is why why-based leadership often needs help.

Why-based leadership can fail when markets and crises evolve quickly, or disruption occurs suddenly and without warning. A tendency exists for established purposes to cling onto even when emerging signals indicate transformation is required, so a great why-based leader must know when their motivation needs to shift.

Begin your voyage of why-based leadership today, dear reader! The waves may occasionally be high and winds strong as we explore these uncharted waters - remember our grand map and steady compass of why guide us. So grab your windbreaker, hold onto your hat, and join me as we embark upon this fascinating voyage into why-based leadership's stormy blues and peaceful shallows together!

"What(s)" of Why-Based Leadership

One approach that has gained traction in the vast landscape of leadership theories is "why-based" leadership. This concept centers around the belief that having a clear purpose or reason behind actions helps drive the resiliency, hard work, and commitment required for organizational success.

A practical 'why-based' leader stands apart from traditional leaders by operating based on a profound knowledge of personal and organizational goals, with all decisions and actions connected to these objectives. They articulate these "whys" clearly and passionately to foster an environment where all contributors understand why they contribute to realizing the vision.

The "why-based" leadership style originates from the philosophy of starting with "why," a concept introduced by Simon Sinek in his influential TED talk and book, 'Start with Why.' This leadership approach emphasizes clarifying the purpose, cause, or belief that inspires individuals or organizations to do what they do. A "why-based" leader, hence, not only knows and communicates what they do or how they do it, but vitally, they articulate why. This "why" statement becomes the foundation of their vision, offering a guiding star that directs and motivates team members.

Understanding and embracing the "why" engenders a sense

of purpose in teams, spurring greater loyalty, innovation, and resilience. This leadership style flourishes in environments where intrinsic motivation, creativity, and commitment are crucial for success.

For instance, Apple Inc. exemplified why-based theory under Steve Jobs' leadership. Jobs consistently reiterated that Apple's 'why' was not just to make computers but "to challenge the status quo, to think differently." This mantra guided the company in its extraordinary innovation pathway, from personal computers to iPods, iPhones, and iPads.

Similarly, Elon Musk's Tesla and SpaceX emphasize a strong 'why': providing sustainable energy solutions and colonizing Mars to ensure human survival. This vision has drawn in a workforce deeply committed to these ambitious goals, as seen in their innovative outcomes despite numerous challenges.

Nonetheless, why-based leadership has its limitations. It may not be effective in highly structured, low-autonomy environments where performance is strictly measured and compliance is paramount. For instance, in a military or strict manufacturing setting, the focus often lies on clear instructions and protocols, leaving little room for why-based leadership to bloom.

Moreover, while a compelling 'why' attracts like-minded individuals, it can deter those who do not resonate with the vision. This restricts diversity in thought, potentially leading to an echo chamber or groupthink, which could inhibit creativity and innovation.

85

Developing why-based leadership requires insight, reflection, and skill-building. Leaders should start by identifying their own 'why,' which aligns with their values and passions. This should be an honest and introspective process that does not merely echo a trendy cause but genuinely reflects one's deepest convictions. To help facilitate this process, Sinek's 'Golden Circle' model—starting with 'why,' then 'how,' then 'what'—can be a valuable tool.

Once the 'why' is defined, practical communication skills are essential to articulating this vision in an inspiring and engaging manner. Resources like Toastmasters or public speaking courses can help hone these abilities.

Lastly, leaders must create an environment that supports their 'why.' This includes aligning the company culture, values, and goals with this vision and fostering an atmosphere of empowerment where teams can personally engage with the 'why.' Regular check-ins about the 'why,' recognition for employees who have exemplified it, and incorporating it into ongoing strategic discussions can ensure consistent alignment and engagement.

As we conclude this exploration of why-based leadership, it is essential to highlight that every leadership style has its time and place. While why-based leadership can motivate and inspire, it is also crucial to balance it with the specifics of the operational environment, team diversity and capabilities, and situational requirements.

Autocratic leaders exert tight control over their team's actions and allow little input from team members. Conversely, why-based leadership fosters open dialogue among team members while simultaneously encouraging each member to identify his/her individual "why." Developing this sense of purpose strengthens team commitment and resilience while building extraordinary commitment among teammates.

Democratic leaders encourage group discussion, collective decision-making, and shared responsibility among team members. Although engaging team members with this approach can be desirable, slow decision-making could occur. Why-based leadership eliminates unnecessary distractions by maintaining an eye toward what drives decisions.

Visionary leaders provide clear directions and motivate their followers. In contrast, why-based leaders use clarity of purpose as a catalyst to encourage individual discovery of personal purpose that aligns with organizational mission.

Servant leadership entails serving the team rather than dominating it, while why-based leaders also foster an environment where their followers feel safe. But while both types of leaders promote an environment conducive to development, why-based leadership goes one step further by inspiring a sense of purpose among team members beyond meeting immediate needs.

Transformative leaders share traits similar to 'why-based' leaders when initiating change and encouraging personal growth. Still, their focus differs significantly, as transformative leaders typically only focus on leading teams through significant transitions. In contrast, why-based leaders focus on how the transformation connects to an overarching purpose.

Purposeful leadership, like why-based leadership, emphasizes an organization's collective purpose while helping individuals connect their personal 'whys' to its goal.

At its core, all leadership theories boast unique features and potential positive ramifications; 'why-based' leadership stands out by emphasizing cultivating individual meaning within an organization's mission context and pursuing one's "why" on both an individual and team level is an effective way to foster motivation that could ultimately lead to increased performance and personal fulfillment.

In the ever-evolving leadership landscape, exceptional leaders grasp the significance of connecting with a deeper purpose. Behind every great leader lies a quest for meaning, which fuels their actions and ignites the passion within their team. Why-based leadership delves into the exploration of personal purpose and reveals how aligning it with the goals and aspirations of their team and organization can yield profound results. This chapter unearths the transformative power of finding a meaningful "why" in leadership and the ripple effects it can generate throughout an organization.

Discovering one's purpose is not a linear path but a labyrinth that requires deep introspection and profound reflection. Leaders start by immersing themselves in self-inquiry, peeling back the layers of their identity and beliefs. They delve deep into their core values—the principles that guide their decisions, actions, and interactions. By examining what genuinely resonates with them on a fundamental level, leaders begin to unravel the threads of their purpose.

This inward exploration extends beyond values into the realm of passions and interests. Leaders must recognize their unique skills and talents and how these gifts align with their professional pursuits. With keen awareness, they can pinpoint the activities that fill them with joy and satisfaction, identifying the areas where they can make the most significant impact. Through this self-discovery, leaders uncover their inherent purpose and the driving forces that ablaze their leadership.

Pursuing purpose is not confined solely to the professional domain; it encompasses an individual's life. Great leaders recognize the interconnectedness of various aspects of life and seek to align their personal and professional purposes. They strive to create a harmonious symphony where each note resonates with intention and direction. Acknowledging the interplay between personal values and professional objectives, leaders harness a holistic sense of purpose that propels them forward with unwavering conviction.

Once leaders have gained a clearer understanding of their purpose, the next step is to align it with the goals and values of their team and organization. Purpose alignment is the key to fostering a shared sense of meaning and significance within the collective. It fuels team members' engagement, loyalty, and commitment, as they feel part of something greater than themselves. Purpose alignment transforms mundane tasks into compelling missions and ordinary teams into extraordinary communities chasing a shared vision.

Leaders must build a culture of openness and vulnerability to forge a path of purposeful alignment. It begins by initiating heartfelt and authentic conversations with their team members, where listening precedes speaking. By genuinely understanding everyone's aspirations, values, and motivations, leaders can identify common threads and uncover the intricate tapestry of purpose within the team. Through this collective exploration of purpose, leaders empower team members to connect their work to their personal sense of meaning and fulfill their contributions.

Communication plays a pivotal role in reinforcing purpose throughout the organization. The leader must be the conductor, orchestrating the symphony of purposeful action through articulate and consistent messaging. Frequent reminders and stories exemplifying how the organization's purpose is realized kindle the flames of motivation and inspire team members to make meaningful contributions. Purpose communication is not a one-time event but an ongoing dialogue that breathes life into the organization's purpose, giving it the oxygen it needs to thrive.

Creating a culture of purpose requires leaders to create an environment where individual growth and self-discovery can flourish. Leaders should nurture an atmosphere of psychological safety where team members feel empowered to take risks, experiment, and grow. By encouraging autonomy and innovation, leaders allow individuals to explore their unique talents and strengths, allowing purpose to manifest organically in their work. Leaders should foster curiosity, providing opportunities for continuous learning and development to align personal purpose with the organization's vision.

Furthermore, Why-based Leadership is not about isolating personal purpose but actively supporting each team member in their individual purpose exploration. Leaders should assume the roles of mentor and coach, guiding individuals to uncover their sense of meaning and fulfillment in their work. By investing in team members' personal and professional development, leaders cultivate a deep loyalty and commitment to the organization, propelling it toward shared success.

In conclusion, Why-based leadership is not a mere philosophical concept but a practice that breathes life into organizations. By connecting with a deeper purpose, leaders transcend the realm of tasks and objectives and embark on a transformative journey impacting their team, organization, and society. Discovering and embracing one's purpose as a leader ignites a fire within, radiating a contagious energy that inspires others to tap into their own potential. When leaders lead purposefully, they become catalysts for positive change, unlocking the limitless possibilities within themselves and those they lead.

8

Uniting the Crew: Combined Integrated Leadership Theory

T he Journey:

The light from purposeful leadership has illuminated our path thus far, driving our expedition from merely setting objectives to seeking and actualizing a collective purpose. But as we pause here at the foot of a mighty crossroad, we understand the necessity of looking back and taking stock of the lessons learned from these diverse planes of leadership before stepping into an uncharted galaxy of combined integrated leadership theory. Transitioning from this familiar terrain requires us to remember and reflect upon the mighty threads woven into the fabric of our leadership tale.

Indeed, these luminary and shadowy reflections will become our guiding stars in our onward voyage. Established norms will be tested, outdated practices will be discarded, and every voice and every silent echo from past journeys will be heard. Still, a common theme weaves its way throughout our journey:

an imperative understanding that washes over us: a leader's effectiveness is not solely confined to purpose. It thrives in an environment of authenticity. This understanding of truly successful leadership is a dedication to the team and a reminder that the leader eats last. We found our compass bearing towards another crucial stop on our leadership voyage, the voyage to authentic leadership. It serves as a bridge, a beacon nudging us from the shores of purposeful leadership to the emerging territories of combined integrated leadership theory.

Authentic leaders remain consistent across trials and triumphs, wear their hearts on their sleeves, and value their values in their actions. Their leadership style is characterized by transparency and integrity, a deeply rooted sense of self, and an unwavering commitment to fostering an environment of trust.

At the core of authentic leadership is the understanding that the leader ensures the team's welfare first. Like a diligent captain who stands steadfast until every crew member has safely left the ship, a leader visualizes the end not as a personal triumph but as the collective victory of their team. Hence, the team's success becomes indistinguishable from the leader's success.

This approach to leadership serves as a powerful transition from purposeful to combined integrated leadership theory. Authentic leadership assimilates the 'why' of the purpose and combines it seamlessly with an unwavering dedication to the team. It forms the undercurrent on which the structure of the integrated leadership theory is built.

We journey beyond tried theories and safe harbors towards an amalgamated model of leadership—a theory that aligns multiple facets of leadership into a comprehensive, resilient, and responsive strategy. Yet, as we stand on this threshold, staring ahead into what lies beyond, we offer a moment to reminisce about the journey that brought us here.

This is our launchpad for ascension into an all-integrative, robust, and innovative leadership paradigm. Once more, voyagers, let's steel ourselves to set sail, powered by the wisdom of our journey and inspired by the intrigue of unexplored potential. As we close our delve into authentic leadership, we stand poised on the brink of a new horizon. We see integrating the features of our leadership voyage as the amalgamation of all that we have learned and yearned for into an innovative leadership perspective.

A Glimpse at the Destination:

As our extraordinary voyage of leadership ends, dear reader, this has not just been another meander through dense jungles of leadership ideology; instead, this has been an exploration of uncharted territories, exploring its mystifying realms. Imagine sailing into an open sea of leadership energy—the Combined Integrated Leadership theory (CIL).

Our journey of discovery involves weaving together various leadership styles—autocratic, democratic, visionary, why-based, and servant leadership styles, as well as transformative ones—into an inclusive, multifaceted theory that unites them all.

Why explore this unfamiliar terrain? The ideal leader is no dream; their existence looms large over the horizon—the essence and heart of our Combined Integrated Leadership theory.

This theory isn't just another addition; it represents an amalgamation of strengths, knowledge gained from history and contemporary events, and some form of predictive thinking for future leadership. Inspiration comes from autocratic decisiveness, democratic inclusivity, visionary foresight, servant-minded humility, transformative adaptability, purposeful dedication, and why-based curiosity.

However, suggesting that CIL provides a panacea for all leadership difficulties would be an injustice and a fantasy. While it carries all the strength of an eagle's wingspan and wisdom of an owl's mind, as well as grace from a dove's soft feathers, its integrative nature means it sometimes struggles to keep up with itself as it navigates a multidisciplinary approach; moreover, its integrative principles may even conflict with conflicting principles of parent theories, at times requiring additional directness due to its pursuit of balance.

Are you in need of agile decision-making skills now? Leverage the CIL's autocratic element to foster innovation and diversity of ideas, utilize its democratic and visionary aspects to drive transformation within resistant cultures, and rely on its transformative, purposeful, and why-based fabric of methodology.

CIL excels in environments that value flexibility, comprehensiveness, and an adaptive problem-solving approach. However,

95

it may prove less effective in rigidly structured organizations or situations requiring one-sided guidance.

So put on your explorer's hat, buckle your boots, and step aboard this ship as we explore the undulating currents and bracing winds of leadership. Eyeing the horizon, we journey toward the dawning light of Combined Integrated Leadership theory! Prepare for a thrilling, challenging, and enlightening voyage ahead—join us on this transformative adventure!

The "What(s)":

Leadership can be like an ocean, full of calm periods, stormy waters, unexpected course changes, and surprising discoveries. While the perfect storm or ultimate treasure has yet to be unearthed, Combined Integrated Leadership theory provides an insightful understanding that may become your haven and source of wisdom.

The Combined Integrated Leadership theory blends the best ideas from different leadership styles: autocratic, democratic, visionary, servant, transformative, purposeful, and why-based. By harmoniously merging these styles, leaders can bring out the best in themselves and their teams. Let's embark on this adventure:

Although often maligned for their rigidity, autocratic leadership styles can be helpful training wheels. By providing clear command and direction during high-stress situations where deliberating with every team member may take too much time, autocratic leadership styles provide useful training wheels without turning into a dictatorship. In the CIL, we employ this style judiciously so it does not become oppressive.

The democratic style offers a stark contrast, emphasizing inclusiveness and shared decision-making. This style promotes trust between team members while encouraging creativity and giving all participants a sense of ownership. The Combined Integrated Leadership theory upholds this style while noting that too much "democracy" may lead to inertia or "decision paralysis."

Next, we move toward visionary leadership styles. Visionary leaders guide their teams' course, inspiring them to work towards it with passion and dedication. Their stories often create a passion within an audience; visionaries can compel teams forward despite the difficult waters ahead. Within Combined Integrated Leadership theory, this approach forms part of its core principles, as inspired teams work better than uninspired ones.

Steering toward servant leadership reveals a style centered on meeting the team's needs. Servant leaders act as the ship's rudders, steering their team toward success while safeguarding their well-being. Combined Integrated Leadership theory embodies "Sailing the Winds of Why," prioritizing team member needs before our own and keeping everyone motivated and nourished throughout the journey ahead.

The transformative style is like an adaptable sea creature; it adapts to different situations quickly. This approach promotes change by setting high expectations and driving members beyond them, which may overstretch team dynamics if left unchecked; however, CIL incorporates it to foster innovation and growth.

Purposeful leadership adds depth and direction to this exploration, providing motivation, commitment, and job satisfaction—essential for job satisfaction and team productivity. Combined Integrated Leadership theory uses this leadership style to guide teams toward their 'North Star.'

Finally, there is why-based leadership. This style serves as a road map, highlighting the reasons behind every journey and adding context and significance to decision-making processes. Combined Integrated Leadership theory also emphasizes this by advocating that every decision aligns with an underlying purpose.

Although the Combined Integrated Leadership theory strives to combine the best from different worlds, we must acknowledge that leadership is unpredictable like the sea itself; no single path leads to successful leadership success; each leadership style possesses its advantages and disadvantages that adapt to specific circumstances.

Beginning the Combined Integrated Leadership theory voyage is a courageous exploration to find balance. As it unites different leadership styles, the theory reminds us that outstanding leadership requires adapting your sails according to winds, currents, and crew needs—something this theory endeavors to do. At its heart lies the "why," an essential force driving our ship forward and providing a beacon to guide us during stormy waters of leadership—this theory forges new pathways into its depths while exploring its mysteries with open eyes and an ever-ready compass!

At dawn on our journey, we gaze across leadership theory's expansive and varied terrain. We've traversed autocracy's sternly unforgiving dictations while enjoying democracy's communal springs; bathed in servant leadership blessings while blooming within transformational leadership's cocoon; flourished under purposeful leadership guidance before rising to our final peak and coming face-to-face with its unifying framework, Combined Integrated Leadership theory, as our goal.

This highly captivating model does not signal the end of our journey; on the contrary, it provides us with an invaluable tool and rallying cry in pursuit of inspired and effective leadership.

Our new trail, the Combined Integrated Leadership theory, is more than just a mix-and-match of existing paths. Instead, it represents a harmonious celebration of all its predecessors' best features, simultaneously uniting and transcending them. It cultivates the decisiveness of an autocratic leadership style, radiates the inclusivity of the democratic style, upholds the humility of the servant style, champions the vision of the trans-formational style, and echoes the authenticity of purposeful leadership styles to form one comprehensive theory.

At its core, however, lies a fundamental truth that underlies and illuminates Combined Integrated Leadership theory: leaders are created for and by their teams, driven by shared goals and ambition. A leader's most significant victories should reflect in their team's triumphs; their successes should feel like whispers of team development, while their goals mirror those of team ambitions.

While this chapter marks an arrival with the Combined Integrated Leadership theory's reveal, it should not be seen as the end. Instead, it serves as an invitation to see leadership not as an ultimate destination but as part of our shared journey that both molds and unites us, giving purpose and direction, but not as an endpoint on its journey.

So, as we stand on the precipice of this uncharted territory, one truth remains firm: our journey never truly ends. Leaders equipped with an integrated compass must traverse deeper waters, ascend higher mountains, and, most importantly, carry their teams forward. They should wake each morning vowing to serve more thoroughly, understand, and inspire deeper than before; their quest won't stop here!

We have no doubt reached the concept of Combined Integrated Leadership, but our journey does not stop here; instead, it extends into the past and even further ahead toward an ideal of ancient and revolutionary leadership. Dear reader, your journey may never end—for we do not represent an endpoint but instead strive to enrich, inspire, and lead in every step forward.

CIL is a beacon of unity and collaboration in the vast ocean of leadership theories. It combines the best elements of various leadership approaches, creating a comprehensive framework for guiding and galvanizing a crew toward a common purpose. However, the Combined Integrated Leadership theory recognizes that no single leadership style can effectively address the complexities and intricacies of leading a diverse team. Instead, it advocates for a flexible and adaptive approach, drawing from different leadership models based on the specific needs and dynamics of the crew.

One key tenet of the Combined Integrated Leadership theory is that leaders should adopt a situational leadership approach. This means tailoring their leadership style to the individual and the situation. A skilled captain understands that different crew members have different motivations and varying levels of competence and commitment and thus require different levels of guidance and support.

Kenneth Blanchard and Paul Hersey's situational leadership approach offers instructions on how leaders can modify their leadership style in response to the crew members' readiness levels. The theory suggests four primary leadership styles: directing, coaching, supporting, and delegating. This allows leaders to assess the competence and commitment of their crew members and choose an appropriate leadership style that best fosters their development.

For example, a crew member who is new to a task and lacks the necessary skills may require a directing style of leadership, where the leader provides clear instructions and closely supervises their progress. On the other hand, an experienced crew member who is highly committed to their work may benefit from a delegation style, where the leader entrusts them with autonomy and decision-making authority.

Another crucial element of Combined Integrated Leadership theory is the integration of transformational leadership principles. Transformational leaders inspire and motivate their crew members, challenging them to exceed their expectations and achieve greater heights while always being there to provide support. By fostering a culture of innovation, creativity, and personal growth, transformational leaders encourage the crew to unite around shared values and vision.

Transformational leaders embody charisma, vision, intellectual stimulation, and individualized consideration. They establish a powerful connection with their crew through charisma, inspiring trust, and loyalty. They articulate a compelling vision, painting a picture of the future that resonates with the crew's aspirations. This vision is a guiding light, motivating the crew to work towards a common goal.

Intellectual stimulation is another vital component of transformational leadership. By encouraging creativity and innovation, leaders challenge their crew members to think outside the box, fostering an environment where new ideas and solutions flourish. This leads to better outcomes and empowers crew members, making them feel valued and invested in the team's success.

Equally important is individualized consideration, where leaders genuinely care about the well-being and development of their crew members. They take the time to understand their individual strengths, weaknesses, and aspirations, providing support and guidance tailored to each person's needs. This personalized approach builds trust and fosters a sense of unity within the crew.

CIL minded leaders prioritize active listening, seeking to understand the perspectives and concerns of their crew members. They provide the necessary resources and support for their crew's success, removing obstacles and promoting a positive work environment. Furthermore, they empower their crew members by delegating decision-making authority, fostering a sense of ownership and investment in the team's goals.

Furthermore, the Combined Integrated Leadership theory highlights the significance of communication and collaboration in uniting a crew. Effective leaders understand the power of open and transparent communication, creating an environment where ideas are shared, problems are addressed collectively, and feedback is valued. By engaging in active listening and fostering a culture of collaboration, leaders can tap into the collective intellect and creativity of the crew, strengthening the bonds that unite them.

One approach that can enhance communication and collaboration is shared leadership. Shared leadership involves distributing responsibility among multiple crew members, allowing for a more collective decision-making process. This fosters a sense of ownership, commitment, and empowerment among the crew members, further cementing unity and collaboration.

In addition to communication and collaboration, Combined Integrated Leadership theory stresses the importance of accountability and authenticity in leadership. Leaders who hold themselves accountable for their actions and decisions, and allow their crew to ask questions and provide input, set the tone for the entire crew. By leading with integrity and authenticity, they inspire trust and loyalty within the crew, fostering a sense of unity and a shared commitment to the team's goals.

Leaders can cultivate accountability by setting clear expectations and standards and reviewing progress toward goals regularly. They must also demonstrate accountability by openly acknowledging mistakes and taking responsibility for their actions. This creates a culture of trust, where crew members feel comfortable admitting their mistakes and learning from them, ultimately working toward continuous improvement.

Successful leaders must be authentic in their interactions with the crew, genuine, true to themselves, and transparent in their actions and communications. This creates an environment where crew members feel safe expressing their thoughts, opinions, and concerns, fostering open and honest dialogue, deepening the connections within the crew, and further cementing their unity.

Moreover, Combined Integrated Leadership theory emphasizes the importance of emotional intelligence in leadership. Leaders with high emotional intelligence can understand and manage their emotions and those of their crew members effectively. This includes recognizing and empathizing with the feelings and needs of their crew, adapting their leadership style accordingly, and fostering emotional well-being within the team.

Leaders with high emotional intelligence are skilled in conflict resolution, recognizing and addressing conflicts before they escalate. They promote a positive and supportive work environment where conflicts can be resolved constructively, leading to stronger teamwork and collaboration. By understanding the emotions and motivations of their crew members, leaders can also tailor their communication and feedback to be more effective and inspiring.

Ultimately, Combined Integrated Leadership theory provides a comprehensive and adaptable framework for leaders to unite their crew towards a common purpose. By drawing from various leadership theories and integrating them into a cohesive approach, leaders can navigate the intricate dynamics of their crew, fostering unity, collaboration, and, ultimately, success. With a situational leadership approach, combined with the principles of transformational and servant leadership, along with effective communication, collaboration, accountability, authenticity, and emotional intelligence, leaders can guide their crew to accomplish remarkable feats together, creating a seamless and synergistic environment where individual strengths combine to achieve extraordinary outcomes.

9

Walking the Plank of Authenticity: Leading by Example

J ourney:

In the vast ocean of leadership, one quality stands above all others: authenticity. It is more than just a buzzword, more than a fleeting trend; it is the cornerstone of effective and meaningful leadership. Authenticity encompasses the genuine nature of leaders, the unflinching commitment to their beliefs, and unwavering dedication to walking with integrity. This chapter delves even deeper into the power of authenticity in leadership and explores the profound impact it can have on individuals, teams, and organizations. We will uncover the essential traits defining an authentic leader and explore strategies to cultivate and enhance authenticity in our leadership journey.

The Essence of Authentic Leadership:

At its core, authentic leadership is not a mask that leaders wear; it reflects their innermost selves. Authentic leaders go beyond surface-level professionalism and embrace vulnerability, transparency, and honesty in their interactions. They possess a profound self-awareness that allows them to understand their strengths, weaknesses, fears, and insecurities, thus enabling them to lead with humility and compassion. By having the courage to be authentic, leaders set an example that inspires others to explore their own truths, open up about their vulnerabilities, and amplify their unique contributions.

Authentic leaders understand the power of openness and trust. They master the art of active listening, genuinely seeking to understand others' perspectives and experiences. By fostering an environment of psychological safety, these leaders create spaces where team members feel comfortable bringing their whole selves to work. Trust flourishes, collaboration surges, and innovation becomes the norm in an atmosphere where authenticity is honored.

The "What(s)" Walking the Plank of Authenticity

To walk the plank of authenticity, leaders must embark on a journey of self-discovery and introspection. It requires peeling back the accumulated layers over the years and revealing the core values, passions, and purposes that define them. As leaders delve into their own unique stories, they find the courage to align their actions, decisions, and behaviors with their deeply held beliefs. This alignment serves as a compass, guiding both themselves and their teams toward a collective vision.

Walking the plank of authenticity also means embracing and

acknowledging that leaders are not infallible. Authentic leaders are fearless in admitting mistakes, seeking feedback, and holding themselves accountable. Demonstrating accountability inspires their teams to do the same, nurturing continuous improvement and growth.

Authenticity is multidimensional, extending beyond personal interactions to encompass leaders' choices and actions. Authentic leaders do not compromise their integrity for short-term gains or popularity. They possess the moral courage to stand firm in their values, even in adversity or pressure. By consistently upholding ethical standards and holding themselves accountable, authentic leaders inspire their teams to stay true to their principles, embedding authenticity into the fabric of the organization's culture.

Cultivating Authenticity in Leadership:

Authenticity can be developed and honed through deliberate efforts and practices. Aspiring authentic leaders engage in a process of self-dedication by actively seeking self-awareness. They embrace practices such as journaling, mindful reflection, and seeking feedback from trusted mentors or peers. These practices enable leaders to gain insight into their authentic selves, identify areas for growth, and make intentional choices aligned with their core principles.

Moreover, personal development and continuous learning play pivotal roles in cultivating authenticity. Engaging in leadership programs, attending workshops and conferences, or participating in relevant courses can expand leaders' understanding of themselves and the world around them. This breadth of knowledge deepens their authenticity by broadening their worldview, enhancing empathy, and facilitating a deeper understanding of the complexities of leadership.

Building a supportive network of mentors, coaches, or like-minded individuals is instrumental in the authenticity journey. Through mutually beneficial relationships, leaders gain invaluable guidance and accountability. These connections provide ongoing opportunities to learn from others' experiences, share challenges and successes, and engage in meaningful discussions about leadership authenticity.

We have explored the complexities of leadership theories, each with its own benefits and applications. Through autocratic leadership, we learned decisiveness and authority; democracy introduced us to consensus-building; servant leadership taught us humility and service; transformative style opened up visionary possibilities; and "why-based" or purposeful leadership stressed guiding values with authentic mission-focused actions.

As our journey concludes, we uncover an exciting framework that unifies these theories: the Combined Integrated Leadership theory. It promises comprehensive, dynamic leadership by merging the best attributes of its predecessors into one exciting concept for today. Although its roots lie deep in history's tapestry of leadership theory, its various strands come together into an exciting fabric appropriate for contemporary life.

But as we use this new map, let us be careful to do so with

humility. While the Combined Integrated Leadership theory offers a holistic view of leadership, no single approach should claim to answer every leadership problem that may arise. Instead, this theory is a versatile toolkit with various principles that adapt well across various scenarios and provide flexibility.

Consistent across every style and theory of leadership lies the significance of the "why." Why do we lead? Answering this question gives leaders an objective lens through which to view their actions and decisions; it directs their decisions, lights their path forward, and attracts followers. Successful leaders have an unambiguous, compelling, and articulated "why" that drives everything about their leadership style or theory.

Combining these theories under a unified umbrella of the Combined Integrated Leadership theory reflects an acknowledgment of leadership's complexity, that leadership is multidimensional and constantly changing, and that optimum leadership involves elements from various styles depending on context, team dynamics, and goal orientation.

Fellow voyagers, I invite you to embrace this new theory and view your tasks, teams, and trials with fresh eyes. Remember: Your journey does not end when a theory is revealed; instead, the true goal lies in discovering and expanding upon your leadership potential, continually fueled by an effort to understand, adapt, and embrace those principles that resonate most for you.

Understand that our discovery of Combined Integrated Leadership theory is only the starting point on an endless journey of self-development and exploration. Continue your journey while courageously learning about all the complexities of leadership and allowing it to mold and shape you. At its heart, leadership transcends theory—a state of constant growth that goes well beyond any one theory.

Leading by example is not a superficial act but a profound commitment to living authentically. Authentic leaders navigate the vast seas of leadership with resolute sincerity, inspiring others to bring their authentic selves to work and fostering a culture defined by trust, innovation, and personal growth. By walking the plank of authenticity, leaders create a ripple effect that extends far beyond their immediate sphere of influence, leaving a legacy of positive impact and genuine connection. Authentic leadership is the compass that guides individuals, teams, and organizations toward their highest potential, setting the stage for profound transformation and sustainable success.

10

Building a Solid Vessel: Creating a Culture of Trust

I n the vast and ever-changing ocean of leadership, one of the most critical elements for long-term success is the establishment of a culture of trust within your team. Trust acts as the sturdy anchor that holds teams together through both calm waters and stormy seas, ensuring that every member feels valued, supported, and empowered to contribute their best. Building solid shipmates goes beyond a mere metaphor; it encapsulates the essence of fostering strong, collaborative, and resilient teams.

Trust, however, is a multifaceted concept that requires a comprehensive understanding and a continuous effort to cultivate. It is not achieved through a singular action or a fleeting moment; instead, it is an ongoing process that demands consistent dedication and deliberate actions from leaders.

Effective leaders know that building trust begins with leading by example. They become beacons of integrity, embodying the values and ethical standards they expect from their team. They demonstrate authenticity, transparency, and consistency in their words and actions, earning the trust of their shipmates. These leaders understand that trust is a two-way street, and they actively communicate openly and honestly, sharing their vision, goals, and expectations with their team members. These leaders foster a culture where trust and collaboration flourish by involving their shipmates in decision-making processes, seeking their input, and valuing their perspectives.

Reliability is another crucial aspect of building trust. Leaders committed to cultivating trust consistently deliver on their commitments and follow their promises. This reliability extends beyond individual tasks; it encompasses creating a work environment that is supportive, equitable, and built on mutual dependability. Trust flourishes when shipmates can rely on one another's competence, accountability, and support, forming the bedrock of a high-performing team.

Open and honest communication is paramount for establishing and nurturing trust. Leaders must foster an environment where shipmates feel safe and empowered to voice their opinions, ask questions, and provide meaningful feedback. They create spaces for dialogue, actively listen to their team members, and genuinely consider their perspectives. By encouraging open communication and actively seeking input, leaders signal that all shipmates' voices are valued, fostering trust and allowing each individual to contribute their unique insights and expertise.

Building trust also involves recognizing and leveraging the strengths of individual team members. Authentic leaders understand that every shipmate brings unique skills and experiences. They provide regular feedback and meaningful recognition, highlighting each member's specific strengths and contributions. Doing so empowers their shipmates to excel, fostering a sense of accomplishment and building confidence in their abilities. Trust thrives when shipmates feel seen, appreciated, and part of a purposeful collective.

Consistency is essential to building and maintaining trust. Leaders must demonstrate consistency in their actions, decisions, and treatment of their shipmates. Inconsistencies and favoritism erode trust, causing fractures within the team. Leaders establish a fair and trustworthy environment by setting clear expectations and holding everyone accountable to the same standards. Consistency also extends to addressing conflicts and challenges promptly. Leaders must actively facilitate open and respectful dialogue, seeking fair and beneficial resolutions for all parties involved. By addressing conflicts with transparency, empathy, and a focus on seeking mutual understanding, leaders demonstrate to their shipmates that their concerns are heard, valued, and addressed appropriately.

Furthermore, leaders must ensure that trust extends beyond the boundaries of the immediate team and permeates throughout the broader organization. They foster collaboration and communication across departments, levels, and geographical locations, creating an environment where trust and cooperation can flourish, leading to overall organizational success. This might involve facilitating cross-functional projects that encourage knowledge sharing, cultivating a culture of mentorship, or establishing platforms and channels for collective learning and support. By encouraging collaboration outside immediate team boundaries, leaders broaden perspectives, build critical relationships, and strengthen the bonds of trust across the organization.

Building a culture of trust requires time, effort, and intentionality. It demands that leaders constantly reflect on their behaviors and strive to improve while supporting and empowering their shipmates to do the same. By privileging the cultivation of trust, leaders create a solid foundation on which their teams can grow, thrive, and face any challenge that comes their way. This culture of trust fosters a profound sense of loyalty, commitment, and belonging among shipmates, enhancing engagement and propelling overall team performance to new heights.

In conclusion, a culture of trust acts as the compass that guides successful leadership. Leaders who lead by example, foster open communication, recognize individual strengths, maintain consistency, address conflicts promptly, and extend trust across the organization build solid shipmates who navigate the complex waters of leadership with unwavering confidence and resilience. Building trust is ongoing, but its rewards are immeasurable. A team that works harmoniously achieves remarkable outcomes and continues to grow in strength, unity, and enduring success.

11

Weathering the Storms: Resilience in Leadership

In the unpredictable seas of leadership, storms are bound to arise. Resilience in leadership is the ability to weather these storms, adapt to challenging circumstances, and emerge even stronger. Leaders must cultivate resilience within themselves and inspire it in their teams.

Resilience begins with a mindset that embraces challenges as opportunities for growth. Obstacles don't demotivate or overwhelm resilient leaders; they serve as valuable teaching opportunities that develop their skills and character. This mindset is rooted in optimism and a belief in one's own capabilities. By adopting a growth mindset, leaders can reframe setbacks as stepping stones toward success, empowering themselves and their teams to persevere in adversity.

Resilient leaders maintain a calm and composed demeanor during crises or adversity. They understand that their emotional state sets the tone for the entire team, and as such, they strive to exude confidence and stability. By remaining composed, leaders reduce fear and panic among their team members, allowing for more rational decision-making and effective problem-solving. They actively seek opportunities to motivate and inspire their teams, reminding them of their collective strength and ability to overcome challenges together.

Building resilience also requires a willingness to adapt and be flexible. Rigid and inflexible leaders will likely be left behind in rapidly changing environments. Resilient leaders understand that adaptability is essential for survival and growth. They stay attuned to emerging trends and market shifts, constantly scanning the horizon for potential threats and opportunities. By encouraging a culture of adaptability within their teams, leaders empower their members to embrace change and proactively identify innovative solutions. They nurture a learning mindset encouraging curiosity and experimentation, enabling their teams to thrive in dynamic and uncertain circumstances.

Additionally, resilience is cultivated by nurturing a positive and supportive environment. Resilient leaders recognize the power of emotional intelligence, empathy, and compassion. They create a safe space where team members can voice their concerns, share their ideas, and seek support without fear of judgment or retribution. By fostering open communication and active listening, leaders encourage collaboration and innovation. They understand that a cohesive and well-connected team is better equipped to weather storms and find collective solutions to challenges.

Resilient leaders understand the importance of self-care for themselves and their teams. They prioritize their physical and mental well-being, recognizing that they can only lead effectively when healthy. They encourage their team members to balance their lives, promoting a culture that values work-life integration, adequate rest, and self-reflection. By modeling self-care practices and providing resources for mental health and stress management, leaders demonstrate their commitment to their team members' holistic well-being.

Leaders who weather storms must remember to celebrate small victories along the way. Recognizing progress and acknowledging the efforts of their team members boosts morale, motivation, and resilience. A leader's genuine appreciation and gratitude for their team members' hard work and contributions fosters a sense of belonging and purpose. Leaders reinforce their teams' resilience by celebrating milestones and encouraging continued growth. They understand resilience is about bouncing back from setbacks, learning from them, and recognizing the progress made along the journey.

In conclusion, resilience in leadership is vital for navigating the storms that arise. Leaders must cultivate a growth mindset, maintain composure during times of crisis, adapt to change, foster a supportive environment, prioritize self-care, and celebrate achievements. By embodying resilience, leaders inspire their teams to overcome adversity, adapt to change, and steer the ship toward success. With resilience as their guiding compass, leaders can navigate even the most turbulent waters and emerge stronger, more adaptable, and more confident to face future challenges.

12

Charting a Clear Course: Communicating the Vision

I n the vast expanse of leadership, one of the most essential and challenging skills is communicating with a clear vision. As a leader, it is not enough to have a vision in your mind; you must master the art of effectively conveying it to your team and stakeholders. Through this communication, you can inspire and align others towards a common purpose, guiding them toward success.

To set a clear course and communicate your vision, fully understand what you want to achieve. Take the time to clarify your purpose, goals, and values. A solid foundation of understanding will enable you to articulate your vision compellingly and authentically, setting the stage for its successful execution.

When conveying your vision, your words must be concise, articulate, and intentional. Use simple language that people at all levels of your organization can understand. Avoid jargon or technical terms that might alienate or confuse your audience. Remember, the goal is to inspire, not to impress. A vision that is communicated with clarity can become a beacon of hope, guiding your team through uncertainty and motivating them to strive for excellence.

Additionally, consider the power of storytelling in communicating your vision. Humans are wired to connect with narratives, and stories uniquely engage emotions and imagination. Share examples or anecdotes that illustrate the impact of your vision and the positive change it can bring. Connecting your vision to real-life experiences makes it more relatable and tangible for others, enabling them to visualize the possibilities and align their efforts accordingly.

Tailoring your message to different audiences is vital to communicate your vision effectively. Recognize that different individuals and groups may have varying perspectives, interests, and priorities. Adjust your communication style and emphasize the aspects of your vision that resonate most with each group. Customize your approach considering their backgrounds, values, and aspirations, making them feel the vision is relevant and meaningful to their personal and professional growth.

Furthermore, communication should always be a two-way street. Encourage feedback and engage in open dialogue with your team and stakeholders. Actively listen to their thoughts, concerns, and ideas. Seek to understand and consider their perspectives when reinforcing and communicating the vision. Creating a safe and inclusive space for meaningful conversations demonstrates that you value their input and are open to collaboration. This fosters a sense of ownership and commitment in those involved, making them more likely to actively contribute towards turning the vision into reality.

Moreover, as a leader, it is essential to consider the different modes of communication that can be employed to convey your vision effectively. While face-to-face interactions are valuable for building rapport, non-verbal cues, and personal connection, various digital tools can be utilized to reach a wider audience and enhance collaboration. Virtual meetings, emails, video messages, and even social media platforms can all play a role in disseminating your vision and fostering engagement.

Additionally, visual aids can be a powerful tool in communicating your vision. Utilize graphs, infographics, charts, and other visual representations to help individuals grasp the vision's key components and potential benefits. Visuals can simplify complex ideas, create a memorable impact, and facilitate understanding across diverse backgrounds and skill sets.

Lastly, consistent and transparent communication is key to keeping your vision alive. Regularly provide updates on progress and milestones, celebrating successes and addressing any challenges along the way. This transparency fosters trust and keeps everyone aligned with the overall direction. Honest and open dialogue about the vision's implementation fosters a culture of accountability and adaptability, empowering individuals to overcome obstacles and make necessary adjustments to the course without losing sight of the goal.

As a leader, your ability to set a clear course and effectively communicate your vision can make all the difference in achieving your goals. By honing your communication skills, tailoring your message, and fostering open dialogue, you can inspire others to join you on the journey towards success. Remember, a shared vision is a powerful force that can unite and propel a team forward. Embrace the responsibility to communicate your vision with clarity, passion, and purpose and witness its transformative impact on individuals, teams, and organizations.

13

All Hands-on Deck: Empowering Teams

I n today's dynamic and interconnected world, collabo-rating effectively and empowering teams is paramount to achieving success. As a leader, you understand that true strength lies not in individual brilliance but in your team's collective effort and talents. This chapter delves deeper into the strategies, principles, and practical aspects of empowering teams, nurturing a collaborative culture, and achieving remarkable results on the deck.

Building Trust: Building a solid foundation of trust is the cornerstone of empowering teams and fostering collaboration. Trust creates an environment where open communication, vulnerability, and mutual respect can thrive. Cultivate trust, lead by example, and demonstrate integrity in your actions and words. Encourage healthy and constructive conflict, where team members can freely express their opinions and challenge each other's ideas without fear of repercussions. Create avenues for regular feedback and communicate transparently about goals, expectations, and organizational changes. Actively listen to your team members' concerns and suggestions, ensuring their voices are valued and considered. By fostering a culture of trust, you establish the conditions for collaboration to flourish.

Delegating Decision-Making: Empowerment is about granting responsibility and delegating decision-making authority. To truly empower your team, delegate responsibilities and decision-making power based on their capabilities and expertise. This allows them to take ownership of their work and fosters a sense of autonomy, accountability, and confidence. Encourage your team members to evaluate alternatives, make informed decisions, and face the consequences of their choices. Provide them context, guidance, and support, but avoid micromanaging or overburdening them with excessive direction. By allowing them to contribute to the decision-making process, you tap into their unique perspectives and expertise, leading to more effective collaboration and innovative outcomes.

Encouraging Diverse Perspectives: Collaboration thrives when diverse perspectives are embraced and valued. As a leader, it is vital to create an inclusive environment where team members feel safe expressing their thoughts and ideas, regardless of their background or rank. Encourage open dialogue and actively seek out diverse viewpoints. Recognize that differing opinions, experiences, and expertise can enrich discussions, spur creativity, and yield more robust solutions. Foster an atmosphere of psychological safety where individuals feel comfortable taking risks and challenging the status quo without fear of judgment or retribution. Additionally, it creates opportunities for cross-functional collaboration, encouraging team members from different departments or areas of expertise to work together. By fostering an environment of inclusivity, you empower your team members to collaborate authentically and leverage their collective intelligence.

Providing Resources and Support: Empowering teams requires providing them with the necessary resources, support, and opportunities for growth. Ensure your team members can access the tools, training, and information they need to excel in their roles. Establish ongoing communication channels to address their concerns, offer guidance, and provide mentorship. Recognize and address any barriers that hinder collaboration, whether related to workload, technology, or interpersonal dynamics. Streamline processes, invest in technology platforms that enhance collaboration, and foster cross-functional knowledge sharing. Encourage a culture of continuous learning where individuals are supported in their professional development goals. Providing the right resources and support empowers your team to collaborate effectively and navigate challenges confidently and competently.

Recognizing and Celebrating Achievements: Recognition is a powerful motivator and reinforcement for collaboration and empowerment. Acknowledge and celebrate individual and collective achievements. Express genuine appreciation for your team members' commitment, effort, and outcomes. Celebrate milestones, breakthroughs, and continuous improvement. Foster a culture of gratitude and recognition where team members are encouraged to acknowledge one

125

another's contributions. This can be done through regular team meetings, public appreciation, or even small gestures such as handwritten notes of thanks. By recognizing their contributions, you validate their efforts and inspire them to go the extra mile, strengthening the collaborative spirit within your team.

Continuous Improvement: Empowering teams is an ongoing process that requires a commitment to continuous improvement. Encourage your team to adopt a growth mindset and seek personal and professional development opportunities. Provide regular feedback, encourage constructive critique, and celebrate learning from mistakes. Foster a culture of curiosity, experimentation, and knowledge-sharing. Regularly assess and refine your team's processes and workflows to adapt to the evolving needs of your organization. Encourage cross-departmental collaboration and engagement with external networks, enabling your team to learn from others, gain fresh perspectives, and stay abreast of industry trends. By nurturing a culture of continuous improvement, you empower your team to collaborate at their best and navigate the ever-changing waters of success.

Empowering teams and fostering collaboration on the deck demands an unwavering commitment to trust, shared accountability, diversity of thought, resource provision, recognition, and constant growth. As a leader, you are responsible for steering the ship toward a culture of empowerment where everyone's unique strengths and perspectives are embraced and leveraged. Encourage your team to unleash their full potential through open communication, transparency, and a supportive environment. Together, you will triumph over challenges, achieve remarkable results, and testify to the power of collaboration and team empowerment.

14

Junior Officers: Developing Future Captains and Nurturing Growth

J ourney:

As our journey unfolds, let's delve deeper into each leadership model we've explored: autocratic, democratic, servant, transformative, purposeful, and the new Combined Integrated Leadership theory (CIL). To increase understanding and help identify our perfect style of leadership development by further exploring their traits and characteristics while applying critical scrutiny and encouraging personal transformation towards building your leadership style.

Autocratic leaders lead with swift resolve and steady control. To embody this leadership, decisiveness, confidence, and clear, assertive communication, don't veer into authoritarianism! Keep team motivation at the forefront, and balance firmness with empathy for your employees.

Democratic leaders assemble to tap into the group's wisdom,

value diversity, promote inclusivity, and reach a consensus on an issue. Listen carefully, demonstrate patience, and embrace humility while creating an atmosphere that welcomes input to foster vibrant democratic leadership.

The qualities of a servant leader require understanding power as an opportunity for service rather than dominance. To demonstrate compassion, you must cultivate empathy, humility, and total commitment to your team's welfare—an ongoing practice where power meets humility; ultimately, this practice breeds service.

Transformative leaders spark, drive change, and inspire their teams toward a shared vision. Successful transformative leaders cultivate charismatic qualities like vision and motivational abilities while remaining open to change and nurturing adaptability, becoming the source of dynamic inspiration that pushes their teams further than before.

Purposeful (or "why-based") leaders anchor themselves in their purpose and goals for leading. When leading with this mindset, make your authenticity, integrity, and purpose-driven mindset known through actions aligned with values and over communicating your 'why' to foster understanding, commitment, and trust with those you lead.

The Combined Integrated Leadership theory can be seen as an advanced level in one's leadership journey. To succeed at embodying this style, one must be flexible in transitioning between styles based on situations, applications, team dynamics, and tasks or roles at hand - essential considerations are mastering none rather than multiple and knowing when and where each should be applied.

When creating your leadership toolkit, consider these theories, their applications, merits, and intertwining nature. An arsenal explicitly tailored to you would make for an appealing leadership Rolodex; experiment with various approaches to monitoring reactions, feedback, outcomes, and gauge fitment.

Remember that leadership development is an ongoing journey. Seek feedback regularly and be open to adaptation; participate in mentoring, coaching, and leadership training exercises; engage in self-reflection and mindfulness practices; and strive to develop emotional intelligence as part of your leadership development—they all play vital roles in shaping your leadership development.

Our journey, as fulfilling as it has been, encourages lifelong learning—pursuing knowledge, skills, and improvements without ever quenching your thirst for more growth. I urge you to reflect upon, assimilate, and apply what you've learned into action; continue exploring, learning, and leading, for our journey doesn't end here; instead, it continues in its epic voyage of learning.

Welcome to the "What(s) and How(s)": Congratulations on reaching the climax of our quest to uncover the secrets of effective leadership. Seven distinct leadership methods were explored: autocratic, democratic, servant, transformative, visionary, why-based, and purposeful. Each style revealed unique strengths and opportunities with deep roots in leadership possibilities. Now comes an exciting challenge—weaving these disparate threads into an integrative style tailored to your context.

Effective leadership methods center on personalizing an approach that is not solely based on one method but rather employs an eclectic combination explicitly tailored to the organization or group's ecosystem, values, and goals. These methods are adaptable and dynamic, flowing seamlessly into synergistic harmony. The spectrum of leadership is such a broad continuum.

Assess Your Context: Understand your organization's unique characteristics and assess your team members' experience, potential, and aspirations. An autocratic leadership style might work best when high-stakes or time-sensitive situations are at play. At the same time, servant leadership could promote more nurturing environments for development and growth.

Outline Your Essential Why and Purpose: At the core of why-based and purposeful leadership lie its fundamental whys and purposes; these help bring clarity, drive commitment, and create a clear direction for moving forward, offering immense strength for crafting engaging stories.

Combine Styles: Unified leadership does not involve diluting one style for another. Instead, consider it a potent concoction where each component contributes to its collective strength at just the right moment and context. Take, for instance, democratic leadership as fairness combined with a transformative leader's guiding vision, autocratic decision-making strength combined with servant management nurturing the servant's clarity from a why-based perspective, and purposeful leadership forward momentum as examples of such ingredients in action!

Empower Your Team: Help them understand, accept, and implement this unified approach to growth and learning at every level. Encourage feedback while always keeping open lines of communication.

Evolve: As with anything in life, flexibility and adaptability are crucial. Each interaction allows you to flex and refine your leadership approach based on the situation. In some instances, more directive or autocratic approaches might work best, while at other times, democratic or servant leadership styles could yield more fruitful results.

Conduct Regular self-reflection. Take time each day to consciously review your leadership style against its actual outcomes, viewing any success or setback as a source of learning and improvement.

At this end of our exploration of leadership, equip yourself with an effective toolbox for the journey ahead. Leadership comes in many forms—autocratic, democratic, servant leadership, and purposeful are just some of its varieties—each speaking its language but all contributing towards providing guidance.

Leadership theories are among the great pleasures of life because they're not static entities to be applied at once but elements on a palette that can be mixed and matched for tailored results. Here are a few ways these theories can be put to work in tailoring an engaging combination for a particular situation:

Examine Your Organization: Each organization comprises individuals with distinct personalities, motivations, and goals who all come together to form it. Gaining a deep insight into its culture and values is essential to understanding its overall direction.

Assess Your Context: Carefully evaluate the scope and nature of your task before choosing an effective leadership style. A time-sensitive project might necessitate autocratic control, while long-term strategic plans may benefit from democratic input.

Leadership as Service: No matter the combination of leadership styles you adopt, adopting Servant leadership increases personal investment and earns you respect from your colleagues. Embarking on this path allows you to empathize with team members while stimulating creativity - ultimately leading to the establishment of an environment in which teamwork serves each other continuously.

Leverage Transformation: Consider transformative leadership as a way to promote an innovative and flexible culture where new methods, mistakes, and learning from them are valued. This environment supports taking risks while accepting feedback and correction as part of its core principles.

Create a Purpose-Oriented Vision: By initiating an impactful 'why,' you create a purpose-oriented road map for your team with great power over motivation and commitment.

Adopt Intentional Leadership: Drive purposeful leadership, cultivating an in-depth knowledge of your employees' aspirations and weaving them into the organization's goals. When individual pursuits meld seamlessly with organizational ones, synergies become unstoppable, and unrivaled progress is accomplished more efficiently.

As we embark on our leadership voyage, it is vital to remember that its destination is only the start of an unending path of personal and professional growth and transformation.

Thank you for choosing to set sail with us. We are privileged to join you on this incredible leadership voyage, offering new perspectives and insight. As you navigate leadership waters, remember that the heart will always guide you to the true north.

Leadership begins from within; at its heart lie service, transformation, and purpose - with you standing alongside those around you and always keeping empathy, purpose, and ongoing learning at the forefront. There is no predetermined route; instead, it is an ever-evolving journey between yourself, your team, and the environment that defines its character. As we sail, your challenge as a leader is refining and defining a blend of leadership that best serves personal and organizational demands. Remember that authentic leadership sails along with people's hearts; you are not alone on this journey as an authentic leader!

Aren't we on a fantastic journey? From the stunning heights of autocratic leadership to the gentle valleys of servant leadership and transformative leadership's electrifying rapids down to purposeful leadership's tranquil depths - we have come a long way in exploring leadership. On this journey, we recognize that leadership impacts many aspects of life and does not reach a static endpoint. Instead, it's an ongoing and dynamic quest for growth, learning, and improvement, wherein its ultimate destination remains simply an imaginary point on the horizon that keeps us going; its actual worth lies within its journey's traces, bonds formed along the way, and transformations witnessed along its course.

In the ever-changing waters of leadership, the most critical task is to nurture the growth of our team members and develop them into future captains. As a leader, we are responsible for creating an environment that fosters the professional and personal development of those under our guidance.

To begin, it is crucial to identify the potential in each individual and understand their aspirations and goals. Take time to have meaningful and individualized conversations with your team members, allowing them to express their ambitions and discuss their strengths and weaknesses. This will help you better understand their unique talents and areas for improvement, enabling you to tailor development plans to help them grow into future leaders.

One effective strategy is to provide opportunities for skill-building and learning. This can be done through mentor-ship programs, where experienced leaders guide and coach

135

their future successors. Mentoring helps individuals develop the necessary skills, knowledge, and confidence to take on leadership roles. Pairing mentees with mentors who have complementary strengths and experiences can offer a well-rounded development experience. Training sessions and workshops can also be organized to enhance specific skills or introduce new concepts. Bringing in external experts or arranging internal knowledge-sharing sessions can also broaden the horizons of team members and encourage a culture of continuous learning.

Furthermore, encouraging employees to pursue further education, such as attending conferences or workshops or obtaining relevant certifications, demonstrates your commitment to their growth and success. Providing financial support or time off for professional development activities signals the organization's investment in their growth and shows an appreciation for their dedication and ambition.

However, proper growth and development are only partially reliant on external resources. It is equally important to foster an environment that encourages self-reflection and personal growth. This can be achieved through fostering a culture of continuous learning and curiosity. Encourage your team members to engage in self-development activities, such as reading books, attending webinars, or participating in online courses. By doing so, they can expand their knowledge, hone their skills, and stay updated with industry trends.

Encourage individuals to explore different areas of interest, take on new challenges, and continuously challenge themselves to grow beyond their comfort zones.

Another aspect of nurturing growth is providing ample opportunities for individuals to demonstrate their abilities and take on challenging tasks. Delegating responsibilities to your team members empowers them and allows them to apply their skills and problem-solving abilities in real-world scenarios. By offering support and guidance, you provide them with the necessary tools to navigate through any obstacles they may encounter. However, balancing providing enough support and allowing them to exercise their independent decision-making is essential. Please encourage them to take ownership of their projects, learn from successes and failures, and adjust accordingly.

Regular feedback and performance evaluations play a prominent role in nurturing growth. Implement a feedback framework that encourages ongoing communication and facilitates the exchange of constructive feedback between team members. Constructive feedback helps individuals understand their strengths and areas for improvement. It allows them to fine-tune their skills and ensures they are constantly progressing towards their full potential. Encourage a culture of open communication where feedback is welcomed and appreciated, and provide opportunities for individuals to reflect on their progress and set goals for further development. Provide specific and actionable feedback that focuses on behavior and results rather than personal traits.

Furthermore, recognizing and celebrating achievements reinforces positive behaviors and motivates continued growth.

Acknowledge the accomplishments of your team members publicly and provide them with opportunities to showcase their work. This boosts their confidence and inspires others to strive for excellence. Celebrate significant milestones and small wins as they contribute to individuals' growth and development. Consider implementing an awards program or other forms of recognition to highlight exceptional performance and foster a culture of appreciation and encouragement.

Encourage a culture of learning and collaboration within your team. Foster an environment where team members support and learn from each other, creating a sense of camaraderie and synergy. Please encourage them to share their experiences, knowledge, and perspectives. By creating opportunities for cross-functional collaboration, you expose your team members to diverse perspectives and foster innovative thinking. Additionally, organizing regular team-building activities or ideation sessions stimulates creativity and strengthens the bond between team members. Implementing technology and tools that facilitate knowledge-sharing and collaboration can further enhance learning and teamwork within your organization.

Lastly, be a role model for growth and development. Show your team members that you are constantly striving to improve yourself. Share your own experiences and the lessons you have learned throughout your journey as a leader. Lead by example and demonstrate a growth mindset, embracing challenges and seeking personal and professional development opportunities. Encourage a culture of learning from mistakes, seeking feedback, and being open to change. Demonstrating your dedication to continuous improvement creates an environment where everyone feels inspired and motivated to grow.

Remember, nurturing growth requires patience, empathy, and a genuine desire to see others succeed. By investing in the development of your team members, you not only ensure the future success of your organization but also create a legacy as a leader who genuinely cares about the growth and well-being of those they lead.

So, set sail on this nurturing growth journey and watch your team members transform into capable and confident captains, ready to navigate their own ships.

15

Steering Through Rough Waters:
Adapting to Change

The Journey

As our narrative continues, we find ourselves aboard the "SS Leadership," a symbolic vessel christened testament to the journey that leadership truly is. Captain Elara stands at the helm, her gaze is steely, her palms instinctively moving over the familiar grooves of the ship's wheel. As she navigates the vast oceanic expanse, she understands the tranquil waters beneath the hull can rapidly churn into treacherous swells.

Captain Elara resonates as the epitome of a leader. She is not just guiding the ship, but with it, her dedicated crew of diverse talents. Together, they face the encompassing water—a representation of change in its natural, wildly unpredictable essence. Captain Elara acknowledges change not as a disruptive storm but as an ocean full of possibilities.

Her leadership echoes the Combined Integrated Leadership theory. Her ability to steer, adapt, and change course based on situational factors is her compass, guiding the SS Leadership through choppy waters. Transforming unwavering autocracy into warm democracy, purposeful direction into an altruistic servant's care, and evolving into a visionary's sight, she navigates the ship seamlessly, never letting the transformative waves tip the boat.

In this chapter, we will follow Captain Elara's expedition through the volatile ocean of leadership. How does she adjust the sails when the winds of organizational change blow unexpectedly? How does she keep the ship steady while crossing the treacherous waters of market fluctuations? We unravel these answers, gaining insight into how a leader's agility, perseverance, and bravery navigate the murky waters, leading the ship and the team to the harbor of success.

Prepare for a voyage through the study of adaptation as we delve into the uncharted waters of change and leadership. Here, you will learn to anticipate and prepare for the unpredictable, harness the power of change, and use it to drive success. Prepare, fellow sailors as we embark with Captain Elara on this enlightening journey, steering through rough waters and adapting to change.

Beginning our sea voyage on the vast waves of leadership, we are prepared to sail through the turbulent waters of various leadership philosophies while aiming for the smooth sail that the Combined Integrated Leadership theory represents. We're armed with a compass of clarity, navigation maps of ability, and the sail of focus, ready to brave unpredictable organizational, environmental, and market changes.

First, let's explore. The seascape of leadership reveals different yet effective modalities of guiding teams. Autocratic leadership, known for its firm mettle, is like the steadfast Atlantic, unwavering in its decisions. Democratic leadership, with its inclusivity, mirrors the warm currents of the Indian Ocean, accommodating the will of many. The purposeful leadership style mirrors the Arctic Ocean, resolute in its mission despite harsh obstacles. Servant leadership is altruism matching the Mediterranean Sea. The Pacific, the largest ocean, represents the visionary leadership mode, sweeping us towards grand, long-term ambitions. At the helm of our voyage is transformative leadership, as dynamic as the elusive Southern Ocean, inspiring change throughout the journey.

Navigating these seas can be demanding. A change in the environment, like a sudden market shift, can feel like a violent storm disrupting a smooth voyage. However, we can ride the waves to calmer waters with the Combined Integrated Leadership theory. This strategy takes the best parts of all the seas. It merges the steadfastness of the Atlantic (autocratic), the accommodating currents of the Indian Ocean (democratic), the resolute nature of the Arctic Ocean (purposeful), the altruistic spirit of the Mediterranean (servant), the grandeur of the Pacific (visionary), and the change-inspiring currents of the Southern Ocean (transformative).

Successfully adopting Combined Integrated Leadership requires adaptability and a thorough understanding of each style's strengths and weaknesses. It means knowing when to steer the ship with a firm hand and when to seek the crew's input on the route ahead. It's about demonstrating genuine care for the crew members' well-being while sustaining the journey's purpose and vision in sight—a constant dance between being decisive, accepting, mindful, altruistic, visionary, and transformative.

Now, why is this important? Our journey is not merely about reaching our destination but also about how we voyage— understanding the "why" behind our actions. A successful leader is merely a compass without its crew; hence, instilling a sense of purpose in each crew member's role is paramount. Inspiring team members to understand their individual contributions toward the greater voyage cultivates a sense of belonging, motivation, and productivity. This involves evaluating the skills, capabilities, and resources available to adapt to the change. By identifying any gaps or areas of improvement, leaders can take proactive steps to address them. This may include training programs, hiring new talent, or reallocating resources to ensure they have the necessary tools and support to navigate the challenges.

Communication plays a crucial role in times of change. Leaders must be transparent and open in their communication with their team. They should provide regular updates, share the reasons behind the change, and clearly articulate the vision for the future. This open dialogue fosters trust, builds confidence, and creates a sense of purpose among team members. Furthermore, it allows for feedback and ideas to flow freely, enabling the team to brainstorm innovative solutions collectively to navigate the challenges.

Flexibility and adaptability are critical traits for leaders when facing change. They must be willing to let go of old ways and embrace new approaches. This may involve redefining goals, restructuring processes, or even transforming the company culture. Leaders need to create an environment that encourages and rewards innovation and creativity. Leaders cultivate a culture of adaptability and resilience by empowering their team members to explore and take risks.

During times of change, leaders need to prioritize their own well-being and that of their team. The rough waters of change can be draining and overwhelming, leading to increased stress and potential burnout. Leaders must lead by example and encourage self-care, ensuring their team has the necessary support and resources to navigate the challenges. This may include providing opportunities for personal development, fostering a healthy work-life balance, and promoting a supportive and inclusive work environment.

Leading through change also requires leaders to be decisive and courageous. Sometimes, tough decisions that significantly impact the organization and its members must be made. Leaders must be willing to make difficult choices and communicate them with clarity and compassion. By doing so, leaders can maintain trust and credibility, even in adversity.

Therefore, leadership development should begin with understanding and developing individual leadership styles. Self-awareness is key, as is understanding one's strengths, weaknesses, and ability to adapt to various situations. It might involve leadership coaching or seeking mentorship from experienced leaders.

Leaders need to remain positive and resilient throughout the change process. They must set an example by maintaining a hopeful outlook and inspiring optimism among their team. Leaders should acknowledge the difficulties and hurdles along the way but consistently emphasize the potential for growth and success. By demonstrating confidence in their ability to navigate through the rough waters and reassuring their team, leaders can instill a sense of trust and motivation in their team members.

Further, it will broaden experiences, increase responsibility incrementally, and network extensively. Welcome opportunities that stretch skills, and be willing to learn. Seek to infuse the principles of servant leadership in daily activities— being selfless, empathetic, and considerate. Additionally, communicate a clear, compelling vision that inspires others towards collective achievement, echoing the principles of visionary leadership.

Combined Integrated Leadership is a dynamic navigation method that, when paired with an agile mindset, can help leaders weather the storm and ride the waves to success. Leadership is a voyage teeming with a depth of experiences, a breadth of insights, and a wealth of possibilities, all revolving around 'why' we chart these waters. After all, we are searching for success and sailing towards an ever-evolving horizon.

145

Adapting to change requires strong leadership skills, a resilient mindset, and an unwavering commitment to success. By embracing change as an opportunity for growth and innovation, leaders can steer their ship through rough waters, emerging stronger and more prepared for the future. Remember, not the calm seas define a leader, but their ability to navigate through the storms and emerge victorious on the other side.

16

Recognizing the Achievements: Celebrating Success

In the fast-paced and demanding world of leadership, it is easy to get caught up in the next goal, milestone, or challenge. However, it is equally important to take the time to pause, reflect, and celebrate the successes and achievements along the way. Recognizing and celebrating accomplishments boosts morale and motivation and fosters a positive and thriving organizational culture.

As a leader, you create an environment where achievements are acknowledged and celebrated. Here are some strategies to help you effectively recognize and celebrate success within your team or organization:

Acknowledge individual and team efforts: Celebrating success begins with recognizing each individual and collective team's efforts and contributions. Take the time to genuinely thank and appreciate everyone's hard work, dedication, and commitment to the shared goals. By highlighting specific accomplishments and the impact they have made, you validate the significance of each contribution. This not only boosts morale but also reinforces the value you place on the efforts put forth by your team.

Acknowledging individual and team efforts also includes recognizing the journey and challenges faced along the way. The path to success is often not linear but filled with obstacles and setbacks. By acknowledging the perseverance and resilience shown by your team in overcoming these challenges, you create a sense of pride and build their confidence for future endeavors.

Personalize the recognition: People are motivated differently, and what may be meaningful for one person may not be for another. Get to know your team members personally and understand their unique preferences. Tailor your recognition efforts accordingly to make them more meaningful and impactful. Some team members may appreciate public acknowledgment, while others prefer a private conversation or a written note. Some might value material gifts, while others may value experiences or additional responsibilities. Understanding their preferences will help you customize your recognition strategy and show that you value and appreciate them as individuals.

Furthermore, personalizing the recognition can also involve considering the diversity within your team. Different cultures, backgrounds, and experiences shape individuals' perceptions and value recognition. It is important to be sensitive to these differences and ensure that your celebrations are inclusive and culturally appropriate. By understanding and catering to the diverse needs of your team members, you create an environment where everyone feels valued and respected.

Create a culture of gratitude: Encourage a culture of gratitude within your team or organization. Foster an environment where expressing gratitude for even the most minor accomplishments becomes a habit. Encourage team members to appreciate and recognize each other, spreading positivity and camaraderie throughout the organization. This can be done through simple gestures like regular team meetings where achievements are shared or implementing a peer-to-peer recognition program where team members can publicly acknowledge each other's contributions. Promoting and fostering a culture of gratitude creates a positive and supportive work environment where success is celebrated genuinely.

In addition to expressing gratitude for achievements, it is equally important to express gratitude for all team member's daily efforts and contributions. Take the time to acknowledge the small wins, the collaborative efforts, and the commitment to excellence. Recognizing the everyday contributions reinforces the value of consistent effort and dedication, ultimately leading to long-term success.

Celebrate milestones and achievements: Set specific milestones and goals towards larger objectives. When these milestones are reached, take the time to celebrate them as a team. This could involve organizing a team lunch or dinner, hosting an awards ceremony, or simply gathering to acknowledge the accomplishments. Celebrating these milestones creates a sense of progress and builds momentum toward achieving the ultimate goal. It also allows the team to reflect on the challenges and lessons learned, fostering a culture of continuous improvement.

It is crucial to celebrate not only the significant milestones but also the small wins. The journey toward a significant achievement is frequently paved with many small victories that deserve recognition. Celebrating these incremental successes maintains motivation and inspires ongoing effort and progress.

Share success stories: Share success stories and examples of exceptional performance with the rest of the organization. Whether through newsletters, team meetings, or company-wide announcements, showcasing outstanding achievements inspires others and reinforces the organization's values and goals. Sharing success stories helps to foster a sense of pride and accomplishment among team members and creates a culture where everyone understands the level of excellence expected. It also serves as a motivating factor for others to strive for their own success.

In addition to sharing success stories within the organization, consider sharing them externally. Celebrating success can be a powerful tool for branding and attracting top talent to your organization. By showcasing the achievements and recognition received, you create a compelling narrative that reflects the positive culture and opportunities for growth within your organization. This can help you attract and retain high-performing individuals eager to contribute to and be part of a successful team.

Provide tangible rewards: Besides verbal recognition and celebrations, consider providing tangible rewards to those who have achieved notable success. This could include bonuses, promotions, professional development opportunities, or even small tokens of appreciation. Tangible rewards not only recognize accomplishments but also motivate continuous growth and success. They show that the organization values and invests in its employees and their contributions, which can lead to increased loyalty and engagement.

It is important to note that tangible rewards should be aligned with the values and culture of your organization. They should be fair, transparent, and based on clearly defined criteria. This ensures that recognition is meaningful and perceived as fair by all team members. Tangible rewards should be seen as a supplement to the overall celebration of achievement rather than a complement to the overall focus of recognition.

Reflect and learn from success: Celebrating success is not just about patting yourself and your team on the back but also an opportunity for reflection and learning. Take the time to assess what worked well, what can be improved, and the lessons learned from the success. This reflection process ensures that achievements are not taken for granted but seen as stepping stones towards further growth and improvement. Encourage open and honest discussions among the team to encourage sharing insights and best practices. By understanding the factors that contributed to success, you can replicate them in future endeavors and continue to drive positive results.

In addition to reflecting on the factors that led to success, it is

151

equally important to analyze any challenges or failures encountered along the way. You can identify strategies to overcome obstacles and enhance future performance by exploring areas where improvement is needed. A continuous learning and improvement culture ensures that celebrating success is not the end goal but a stepping stone toward ongoing growth and development.

Remember, celebrating success is not a one-time event but an ongoing practice. By consistently recognizing and celebrating achievements, you cultivate a positive and rewarding work environment that inspires individuals and teams to reach new heights. Celebrating success catalyzes continued success and is the building block for a prosperous future.

17

Sailing into the Sunset: The Legacy of the Leader

O ur journey into the dynamic and intriguing leadership realm ends not with a dramatic conclusion but instead on the brink of something exciting new, with the Combined Integrated Leadership theory serving as our lighthouse through this vast ocean.

Our theory, an amalgam of all the wisdom we've gleaned on our expedition, should not be seen as an end but as a starting point. Compass rose in hand, eyes trained north; we still have much work ahead. Our journey has only just begun.

Sustainable leadership success lies in mutual growth and the collective achievements that result from its application of Integrated Leadership theory, creating an intricate bond between those being led and themselves that remains ever-evolving and dynamic.

Combined Integrated Leadership's heartbeat is rhythmic and

compelling; leading, serving, and uniting are its defining characteristics. It embodies the belief that leaders' true motivation lies beyond personal achievement; they care more for team success, collective triumph, and a shared joy of achievement than themselves as individual beings. Furthermore, CIL stresses the significance of why, as much as how, when measuring leaders, the success of those they lead accurately measures one's worth as a leader.

Our journey through the realms of leadership has shown us that leadership success isn't something to reach but rather something that must be earned and pursued as a process and goal over time. Leaders should embrace their unpredictable journey with an eye towards growth as more than a mere destination; it should become part of their everyday existence and their lifelong pursuit of discovery, expansion, and evolution.

Indeed, as we conclude our examination of the Combined Integrated Leadership theory, we find ourselves not at an end but at an exciting threshold—an invitation to continue exploring in pursuit of more incredible goodness and greatness, to maintain the flame of curiosity within ourselves while mustering the courage to keep learning, growing, and leading.

This is the strength and promise of the Combined Integrated Leadership theory: it serves as an expression of each leader's passion, courage, and resilience, as well as an invitation for those yet to discover their leadership potential. There is no grand finale regarding leadership; only fresh starts promise more incredible promise than before.

And so we invite you to let go of endings and embrace the endless expanse of beginnings that lie ahead. Welcome to the next step in your leadership journey—an expedition without an endpoint, where each success along the way becomes its own reward. On this leadership voyage, every leader's heart beats with a rhythm that resonates within those they lead and their collective success.

Our destination may be Combined Integrated Leadership, but the journey toward better leadership, purpose-driven service, and collective success of those we lead remains alive and kicking! Let's keep this spirit alive as we explore greater horizons in the future. In conclusion, we encourage Adopting Leadership From the Heart.

As the journey draws to a close, a leader's accurate measure is revealed in the legacy they leave behind. In this final chapter, we explore what it means to sail into the sunset as a leader and their lasting impact on their crew and the world around them.

A leader's legacy is not defined solely by their achievements or the success of their endeavors. It is about the relationships they have built, the values they have instilled, and the inspiration they have sparked in others. It is about the ripple effect of their leadership, spreading far beyond their time at the helm.

In sailing toward the sunset, a leader must ensure their vision endures. This means empowering and developing future leaders who can carry the torch and continue the journey. It means fostering growth and continuous improvement where innovation and adaptation are embraced.

However, sailing into the sunset requires more than just guiding others; it necessitates self-awareness and reflection. Leaders must delve deep into their souls, exploring their strengths, weaknesses, fears, and vulnerabilities. This introspection allows them to understand themselves better and, in turn, better understand those they lead.

To sail into the sunset as a leader also requires recognizing that leadership is not a solitary endeavor. It is about recognizing the contribution of every crew member and understanding that each person brings valuable skills and perspectives to the table. A leader must cultivate an environment where everyone feels appreciated and empowered, fostering a sense of belonging and purpose.

As the sun begins its descent, a leader must be willing to let go of control and trust the abilities of their crew. This is not a sign of weakness but rather an act of empowerment. By stepping back and allowing others to take charge, a leader encourages growth, innovative thinking, and the development of new leaders who can carry the torch into the future.

But sailing into the sunset as a leader is not just about ensuring the ship stays afloat but about leaving a mark on the world. A leader's legacy can be seen through the positive change they have brought about beyond the confines of the ship. It may be in philanthropic endeavors, advocacy for social justice, or contributions to the greater community. A leader's impact in their immediate sphere of influence extends far beyond, leaving a lasting and influential footprint.

156

As the sun continues to dip lower, leaders must confront their mortality and the finite nature of their time on this earth. It is a humbling reminder that life is a fleeting journey, and the legacy a leader leaves behind is what lingers in the hearts of those they have touched. Expressing gratitude and appreciation becomes paramount as a leader reflects on the individuals who have supported and shaped their journey.

In sailing into the sunset, a leader may also realize that their time at the helm is ending. While this can be a poignant moment, it is also an opportunity for celebration. A leader must take a moment to recognize and celebrate their accomplishments and the impact they have made. This acknowledgment is not a self-indulgent act but rather an affirmation of the importance of personal growth and the journey that has shaped them into the leaders they have become.

Embracing vulnerability is essential to sailing into the sunset as a leader. It requires acknowledging shortcomings and mistakes, being open to learning and growth, and allowing oneself to stand authentically in humanity. A leader creates space for compassion, understanding, and forgiveness for oneself and others. This vulnerability strengthens connections and fosters resilience, ultimately leaving a profound impact on the emotional and mental well-being of the crew.

As the sun slowly disappears beyond the horizon, a leader must also contemplate their purpose and the meaning they have derived from their role. The journey's experiences, triumphs, and challenges all contribute to the tapestry of a leader's legacy. It is through reflection on these moments that a leader can distill the wisdom and lessons learned for future generations.

Ultimately, sailing into the sunset as a leader means embracing the fullness of the experience. It is a journey that emphasizes self-reflection, empowering others, having a lasting impact on the world, and expressing gratitude. As the last rays of sunlight fade away, a leader's legacy illuminates the path for others to follow, ensuring a brighter future for all who come after.

18

Afterword

D ear Readers and fellow travelers on the journey to
leadership,

Reflecting upon our remarkable journey together
through this book, I am filled with profound gratitude and
inspiration. Our dedication to helping leaders become all
they can has been a labor of love born out of a genuine belief
in inspired leadership guided by a heart-centered strategy
rooted in "Why." I have witnessed firsthand how this approach
transforms leadership roles for all concerned; now, it is my
privilege to share my reflections with you all.

At its core, leadership is an art that transcends techniques and
strategies. It requires us to connect with our innermost values,
discover passions that drive us, and act kindly toward others.
At every turn in this journey, we have championed harnessing
each leader's full potential to illuminate paths for teams, entire
organizations, and communities.

Leadership from the heart means embracing authenticity, vulnerability, and empathy to foster an environment where people can flourish and reach their full potential. We must remember that our true measure of success should not be measured by simply achieving goals but by positively affecting those we lead. When we approach leadership with compassion and focus on building trusting relationships as our ultimate goals, we create an environment where all can flourish and realize their full potential.

By exploring our "Why" and not being preoccupied with just the "What," we unlock the power to motivate ourselves and others. Finding our core purpose can ignite an internal fire, fueling our actions with meaning and significance. When led with clarity of purpose, leaders become beacons of hope, sources of motivation, and sources of inspiration to those around them.

Let us not forget that leadership is not a solo journey; we embark on it together as part of a community with shared goals. As we work toward promoting heartfelt leadership from within our organizations and communities, let us maintain our vision of supporting each other, encouraging collaboration rather than competition, and empowering every individual leader with authenticity. Since the outset of our journey, our dedication to helping leaders become the best versions of themselves has seen them transform organizations, heal fractured teams, and positively influence countless individuals. This experience strengthens our conviction that leadership from the heart, driven by what motivates us, is always the optimal approach.

At the end of this chapter, I extend my deepest thanks to each of you for being part of my journey and inspiring me with your unwavering dedication to growth, making a positive difference, and leading from your heart. Together, let us continue this transformative path to foster an environment filled with inspirational leaders whose actions touch lives across the board.

Celebrate success and recognize the achievements of your crew. Explore the importance of acknowledgment and celebration as motivators for continued growth and success. In the leadership journey, it is easy to become consumed with the challenges and obstacles that lie ahead. However, stepping back and celebrating the victories along the way is equally important. Recognizing and acknowledging success not only boosts morale within your team but also serves as a powerful motivator for continued growth and achievement.

Celebrating success goes beyond the act of simply acknowledging achievements. It involves creating a culture of appreciation where every triumph, no matter how small, is seen as an essential milestone in the journey toward a shared vision. Every effort made in the journey is a success, and celebrating successes sets the stage for a positive and engaging work environment that inspires and encourages your crew members to give their best.

To effectively celebrate success, it is essential to tailor your approach to the unique dynamics of your team. Understand your team's preferences and motivations, and create meaningful ways to acknowledge their efforts. Personalized recognition can profoundly impact whether it's a handwritten note, a small gift, or a public shout-out during team meetings. By acknowledging the specific contributions of individuals, you show that their efforts are seen, valued, and appreciated.

We have all heard that we praise in public and provide constructive feedback in private. Publicly recognizing individual accomplishments boosts individual confidence and inspires others to strive for excellence. Sharing success stories within the team can be a powerful tool for motivation and learning. Consider organizing periodic team gatherings or award ceremonies to highlight outstanding performance and provide a platform for celebrating achievements. Encouraging team members to share their stories of triumph can foster a culture of inspiration and support.

In addition to individual recognition, it is equally important to celebrate team achievements. When the collective efforts of your crew result in significant milestones or breakthroughs, take the time to honor the collaboration and teamwork that made it possible. This could be through team-building activities, rewards, or even a simple, heartfelt message of appreciation that acknowledges the collective contribution. By emphasizing teamwork and synergy, you create an environment where every team member feels proud and valued for their unique role in attaining success.

Furthermore, celebrate the process, not just the outcome. Recognize the effort, dedication, and resilience demonstrated by your crew members, even when the desired outcome was not achieved. By doing so, you create an environment that supports continuous growth and learning, where failures are seen as opportunities for improvement rather than setbacks. Encourage open discussions about lessons learned from successes and setbacks, fostering a growth mindset within your team.

However, celebrating success should not be limited to just one-off occasions. Make it a regular practice within your team. Create rituals that allow for ongoing recognition, such as monthly or quarterly milestones, birthdays, or anniversaries within the team. Begin each meeting with public acknowledgment of "wins," as that behavior makes it much more impactful when alterations or concerns are needed to be expressed. Establishing a consistent celebration culture reinforces the importance of recognition and fosters a sense of unity and camaraderie among your crew members.

Ensuring that celebrations are inclusive and diverse is critical, reflecting every crew member's unique strength and contribution. Encourage peer-to-peer recognition, where team members acknowledge and appreciate each other's achievements. This promotes a positive and supportive culture and strengthens the bonds within your team. By fostering an environment of shared celebration, you build a sense of collective achievement, where every win is celebrated as a team victory.

In conclusion, celebrating success is more than just a formality. It is a powerful tool for fostering motivation, engagement, and a sense of pride within your team. By recognizing achievements, big and small, and creating a culture of appreciation, you inspire your crew members to reach new heights and continue striving for excellence. So, take the time to pause, reflect, and celebrate the journey so far, for it is in these moments of celebration that you build a resilient and successful team that can conquer any challenge ahead.

Leadership is a privilege, not a right. Leaders are mindful of others successes, not their own, because they realize that their success should be measured by the success of those they are entrusted to lead.

Thank you again for accompanying us on this leadership expedition; we are looking forward to the exciting journeys that still lie ahead.

With profound thanks,

Your fellow traveler on the Seas of Leadership.